Lots and Lots of Candy

by the same author

Miss Patch's Learn-to-Sew Book
Stitch by Stitch: Needlework for Beginners
The Bread Book: All About Bread and How to Make It
Yarn—The Things It Makes and How to Make Them
The Needlework Book of Bible Stories

Carolyn Meyer

Lots and Lots of Candy

Illustrated by Laura Jean Allen

HARCOURT BRACE JOVANOVICH
NEW YORK AND LONDON

To the tasters,
Alan, John, Chris, and Bill

Text copyright © 1976 by Carolyn Meyer
Illustrations copyright © 1976 by Harcourt Brace Jovanovich, Inc.

All rights reserved. No part of this publication may be reproduced or transmitted in any form or by any means, electronic or mechanical, including photocopy, recording, or any information storage and retrieval system, without permission in writing from the publisher.

Printed in the United States of America
First edition
B C D E F G H I J K

Library of Congress Cataloging in Publication Data

Meyer, Carolyn.
Lots and lots of candy.

Includes index.
SUMMARY: A cookbook which supplies recipes for and a history of a variety of candies.
1. Confectionery—Juvenile literature. [1. Confectionery. 2. Cookery] I. Allen, Laura Jean. II. Title.
TX792.M48   641.8′53   76-12483
ISBN 0-15-249400-6

Contents

1
Everybody Likes Candy   7

2
Honey: the First Sweet   11

3
Sugar: News from the East   16

4
Sugar: a Natural Food   27

5
Candy: Chemistry Plus Magic   42

6
Old-fashioned Favorites   49

7
Xocolatl to Chocolate   56

8
World Candy Sampler   73

Index   94

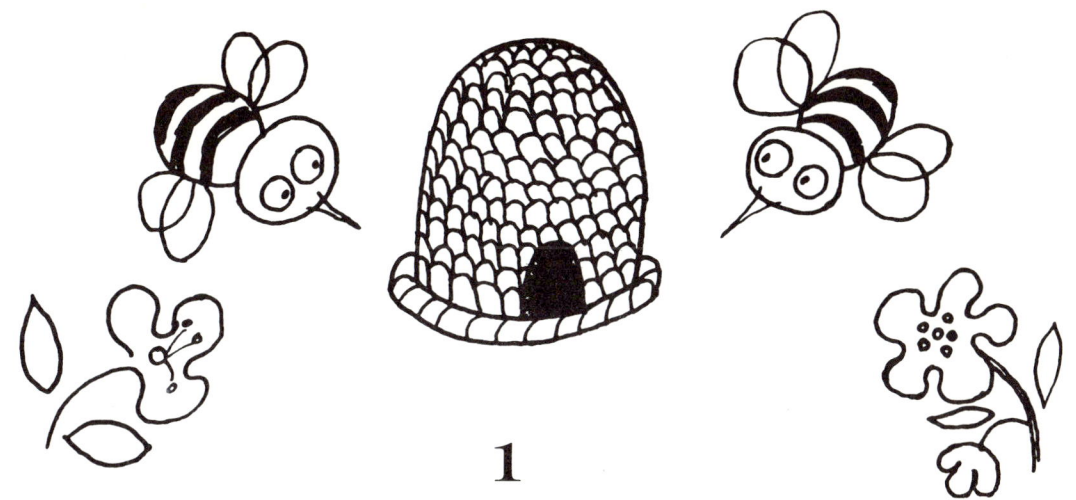

1
Everybody Likes Candy

Candy: a lot can be said about it, but probably the most important thing is that it tastes so good. Almost everybody likes sweet things. Apparently it has been that way since before the beginnings of recorded history, when people first found wild honey and enjoyed the taste. Honey was used to make the earliest confections, or candy, as it is called in America.

Many centuries later people learned to cultivate sugar cane and to extract the sweetness from it. At first sugar was extremely expensive, but as sugar cane production increased, candy became available to everyone. Candymaking was recognized as a craft and sometimes even as an art form.

The next important event was the discovery of chocolate. It was Cortez, the Spanish explorer, who first tasted the Aztec drink in Mexico. Eventually the people of Europe were as enthusiastic about chocolate as they were about sugar.

Candymaking on a large scale began in England, but it was in America that it became a major industry. Each country has contributed to the history of candymaking, and there are said to be *more than two thousand* known varieties of candy. There is a candy to suit virtually every taste: smooth, creamy candies that literally melt in your mouth; chewy candies; hard candies that last a long time. Candies come in many shapes and many flavors: chocolate, vanilla, mint, fruit, licorice, cinnamon, and so on. There are plain candies and candies made with nuts or coconut or peanut butter or fruit. There are simple chocolate bars and elaborate hand-dipped chocolates with rich centers. Candy-munching Americans consume close to eighteen pounds of candy a year per person, two-thirds of it some form of chocolate.

Everybody Likes Candy

Candymaking is part chemistry, part cookery, part craft. All you need for making candy at home is basic cooking equipment: a saucepan and a wooden mixing spoon, plus a candy thermometer. Usually the ingredients are things you have on hand. Some candies are very simple to make—there is scarcely anything you can do to spoil them. Some candies are very complicated and require skill. Most candy falls somewhere in between: not difficult if you follow directions carefully. It's fun to make as well as delicious to eat.

This book is all about candy: its history, traditions, technology, and step-by-step recipes for lots and lots of candy.

What you need to know before you start to make candy

In the old days, candymakers relied on a "simple" test to determine whether the candy had boiled long enough. The cook kept a cup of cold water next to the pot, occasionally dropping into it a bit of the candy syrup. The quickly cooled syrup reacted in certain ways, and experienced candymakers could tell when the candy was done. But many batches of candy were ruined until the cook developed that experience.

The invention of the candy thermometer put an end to the guesswork. Although it costs a few dollars, a thermometer will undoubtedly save you from throwing away many more dollars' worth of ingredients. Except for a saucepan and a wooden spoon (metal may burn your hand), there's little else you'll need in the way of equipment. Use a deep, narrow saucepan rather than a wide, shallow one because then the bulb of the thermometer is always below the surface of the syrup and the syrup will not cook over when it boils up, sometimes to several times its original volume.

Before you use the thermometer, check it for accuracy by putting it in a pan of boiling water. It should register 212 degrees. If it reads higher or lower, figure how many degrees it is off and add or subtract this amount from the temperature given in the recipe.

Be sure to read the thermometer at eye level, and don't try to do anything else while you're making candy. The temperature can change very suddenly.

Certainly the most important thing to remember in making cooked candy is *safety*. The boiling syrup is extremely hot, much hotter than boiling water. Be careful not to let any of it splash on you when you are pouring. And remember that it cools very slowly. You may be tempted to lick the spoon or taste a sample of the candy before it has cooled. Don't do it: you may burn your mouth because the candy that feels warm to the touch may still be very hot inside. Wait until it is completely cool before you sample it, and then you can completely enjoy your first taste of your delicious homemade candy.

2
Honey: the First Sweet

The life of prehistoric man was a day-to-day struggle for survival. Besides finding shelter and protection from wild animals, he had to get food for himself and his family. He was not much concerned with how the food tasted; the important thing was that it be nourishing—not poisonous.

Imagine, then, the pleasure of that person in prehistory who first tasted honey. By some accident he had found the hiding place where the bees had stored their honey. His curiosity aroused, the man of many thousands of years ago reached his hand into the hive, dug out a chunk, and licked the sticky stuff off his fingers. Certainly nothing had ever tasted so sweet. It was worth a few stings to raid the hive and carry the delicious stuff to his companions. They found that it not only tasted good but also gave them energy.

Eventually people in ancient times found that it was not necessary to trust to the luck of finding the honey of wild bees. They developed the science of apiculture—beekeeping. Pictures on the walls of Egyptian tombs of 2600 B.C. indicate that it was practiced at least that long ago.

When things are scarce, they are usually thought to be precious as well. And since good-tasting honey was never available in large quantities, its enjoyment was reserved for the rich and powerful. Honey and the potent drinks made by fermenting it were used for religious ceremonies. It was an offering made to the gods, and it was used at the weddings and funerals of important people. There are frequent references to honey in the Bible: when Joseph's brothers set out for Egypt to buy some grain for their starving people, they took along gifts of honey to sweeten the deal. And when God spoke to Moses from the burning bush, He said that the Israelites would be led out of Egypt "unto a land flowing with milk and honey." There may have been honey in Egypt for the wealthy

Everybody Likes Candy

Egyptians, but there was none for the poor Israelite slaves.

The Egyptians were among the first candymakers. They mixed honey with seeds and fruits, producing very sticky mixtures that they colored with brilliant food dyes to attract attention. In some places in the Middle East, candy is still made in bright colors. In the United States, candy manufacturers design wrappers that catch the eye and identify the product. In recent times of rising prices, these wrappers have also come to conceal the fact that there is not as much candy in the bar as there used to be.

Honey is an excellent sweetener for homemade candy. The honey candies you make today are direct descendants of the candies made thousands of years ago. Here are two basic recipes with several variations. The Honey Balls are uncooked, but the other ingredients keep them from becoming too sticky. Honey-Seed Candy is made by boiling the honey first to thicken it so that, when it cools, it is chewy rather than sticky.

Honey Balls

You will need a measuring cup and spoon, small mixing bowl, rubber scraper, mixing spoon, and:

⅓ cup dry milk powder
⅓ cup honey
⅓ cup peanut butter, either chunky or smooth
¼ teaspoon vanilla
⅓ cup of *one* of these extra ingredients:
   wheat germ
   grated unsweetened coconut (available at health-food stores)
   sesame seeds (available at health-food stores)
   crushed dry cereal
   chopped raisins, dates, or other dried fruit

Put the dry milk powder, honey, peanut butter, and vanilla in the mixing bowl, cleaning the measuring cup with the rubber scraper. Mix them well to form a smooth paste, stirring until the grains of powdered milk disappear.

Add one of the extra ingredients. Or divide the basic recipe in two parts and add two tablespoons of one of the extra ingredients to each part.

Form one-inch balls. Roll the balls in any one of the first four suggested extra ingredients, or leave them plain.

Cover and keep in the refrigerator. The basic recipe makes two dozen one-inch balls; with additional ingredients, it makes about thirty balls.

Honey-Seed Candy

You will need a measuring cup, frying pan, potholder, 1½-quart saucepan, wooden mixing spoon, candy thermometer, baking sheet, sharp knife, wax paper or plastic wrap, and:

> 1 cup sesame seeds *or* ⅔ cup sesame seeds and ⅓ cup chopped nuts
> ⅔ cup honey
> vegetable oil

Put the sesame seeds in the frying pan and heat slowly to bring out their flavor. Stir the seeds with a spoon until they are golden.

Pour the honey into the saucepan. Put the candy thermometer into the saucepan, bring to a boil, and cook to 265 degrees.

Take the pan off the heat. Take out the thermometer and lay it aside. Stir in the sesame seeds or the sesame seeds and nuts.

Grease the cookie sheet lightly with vegetable oil. Pour the honey mixture on it and spread it with the spoon to a thickness of about ⅛ inch.

When the candy has cooled a little, cut it with a sharp knife into bars about 1 inch by 1½ inches. After the bars have cooled completely, wrap them individually in squares of wax paper or plastic wrap. This recipe makes about thirty bars.

3

Sugar: News from the East

"A kind of honey made from reeds" is how Pliny the Elder, a Roman naturalist, described sugar some 2,000 years ago. Pliny, however, probably had no firsthand knowledge of sugar, which was not then available in his part of the world. But he may have read about it in an account written from India by Nearchus, an officer in the army of Alexander the Great. Cultivation of sugar cane and manufacture of crude sugar had been carried on in India for a couple of centuries before Alexander's army invaded the northern province of the Punjab.

The "reeds" are actually tough stalks, sometimes twenty feet high and an inch or two thick, resembling bamboo and full of sweet juice. Workers in the cane fields eat sugar in its crudest form: they cut pieces of cane and chew them. Beginning in India 2,500 years ago, sugar was obtained by crushing the

Sugar: News from the East

cut stalks and boiling the juices to evaporate the water. The dark brown sugar that remained is called *gur*, and the method, the oldest known, is still used in India and a few other countries. But it has been replaced in most of the industrial world by modern refining methods, in which the juice is separated into sugar and molasses in whirling centrifuges.

Knowledge of sugar making spread slowly through the Orient. The Chinese were growing sugar cane in the first century B.C., but it took them some time to learn from their Indian neighbors how to refine it. It was not until about the sixth century A.D. that sugar began to move westward. For over a thousand years, during which sugar had become an important part of Oriental civilization, the Egyptians, Hebrews, Greeks, and Romans ate honey and knew of sugar only by hearsay, if at all. But cultivation finally spread to the eastern Mediterranean. And from there it reached Western Europe in one leap, carried by the Crusaders.

From the eleventh to the thirteenth centuries, European Christians made frequent expeditions to the Holy Land, which they were trying to recapture from the Moslems. There they tasted and enjoyed sugar. When they discovered that it kept them from feeling hungry, sugar became part of their rations. This prac-

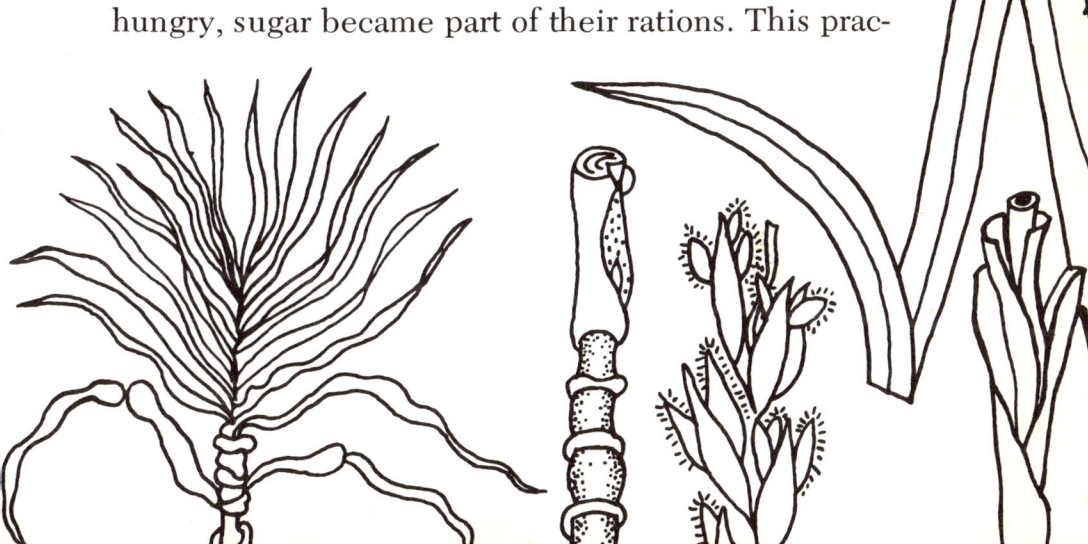

tice is continued by modern armies, which issue candy bars and sugar tablets as emergency rations for staving off hunger and providing the troops with quick energy. When the Crusaders returned to their homes in Europe, they took samples of sugar with them.

One taste was enough. Soon everybody in Europe wanted more. Egypt began to produce sugar, shipping it to Europe by way of Venice. Then the Spanish and Portuguese also began to grow sugar cane, as did people in other Mediterranean countries with warm, moist climates.

Then in 1493, when Columbus made his second voyage to the New World for the Queen of Spain, he took with him some sugar cane and planted it on the island of Hispaniola. The sugar cane thrived, and within a few years Caribbean sugar was being eaten in Spain.

Sugar: News from the East

Sugar cane is highly perishable; once the cane is cut, it must be crushed and the syrup removed the same day. There was not enough native labor on the islands to do all the necessary hard work. Therefore, as a result of the demand for sugar, an ugly new business was born: the slave trade. Among warring African tribes, it was customary for the winners to make slaves of the losers; European slave traders stole or bought the losers and took them in over-

crowded ships to the Caribbean, where the survivors of the long voyage were sold to the owners of the sugar plantations.

As production increased, so did the popularity of sugar. When sugar had first reached Rome, carried by the Crusaders, it was sold by apothecaries, as druggists were called, who prescribed it as a medicine itself or mixed it with drugs to disguise their terrible taste. In the fifteenth century, before sugar was introduced in the Caribbean, it was scarce and extremely expensive; only royalty and nobility could afford it. They used it as a spice to conceal the taste of rotting meat. Even after sugar began to flourish on the islands of the Caribbean, it was still expensive and was sold by the ounce, not by the pound, but by then it was no longer used simply to cover the bad taste of other foods. Candymakers, called confectioners, opened shops that catered to very rich customers. During the seventeenth century, when much more sugar was pouring into Europe, monks and apothecaries began to make and sell candy to the prosperous middle classes. There were also bakers who were permitted to make cakes and other sweets for sale to the public. At first the candies took second place to such big sellers as gingerbread, but as demand grew, some bakers began to specialize in candymaking.

Sugar: News from the East

One of the first sugar candies was *marzipan*, a paste made with finely ground almonds. The Crusaders tasted the candy, which had originated in the Orient, and called it *marchpane*, a name derived from the Arabic word for coins in use at that time. They carried the coin-shaped candy to Italy, where marchpane became a well-liked but very expensive treat.

As marchpane spread throughout Europe, the original coin shape gave way to more elaborate forms, and the spelling changed to marzipan. Certain European cities became famous for their marzipan figures. The city of Odense in Denmark is known for its little pink pigs. In Germany, Lübeck and Königsberg have worldwide reputations for tiny, realistically painted fruits and vegetables. Marzipan is often associated with holidays, and it makes its appearance

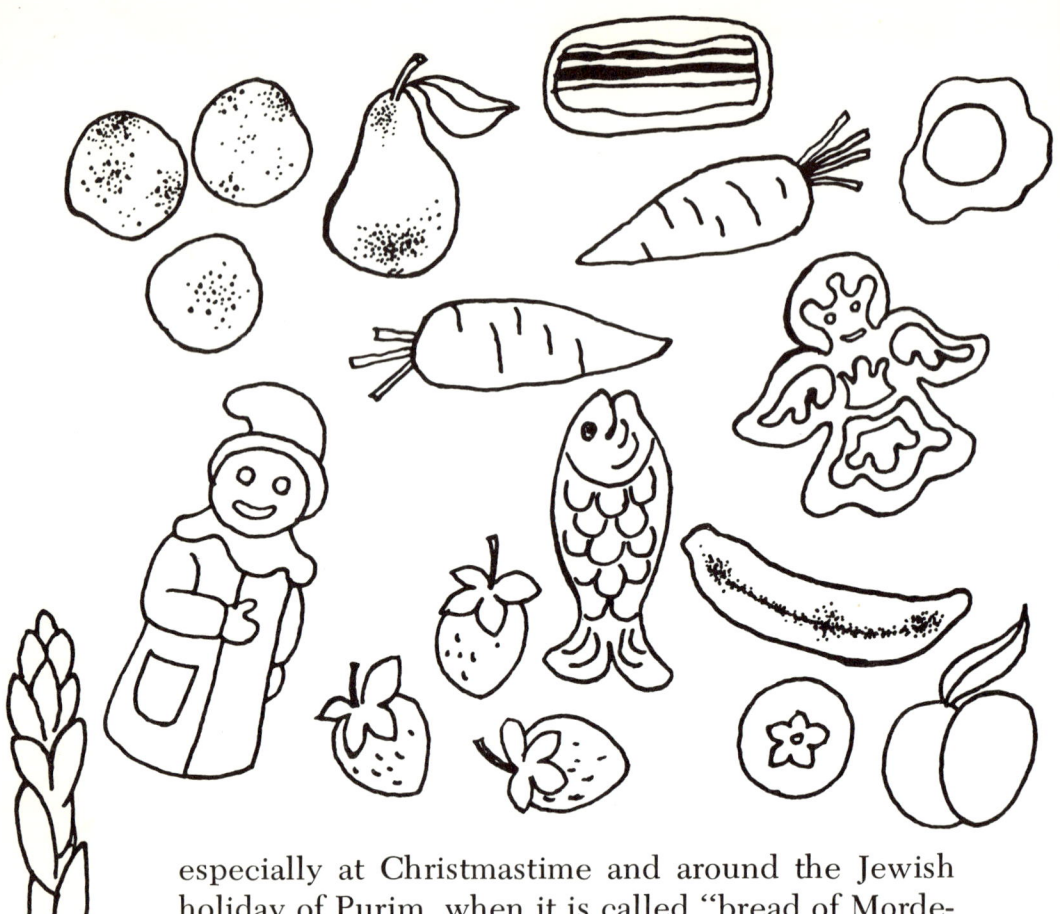

especially at Christmastime and around the Jewish holiday of Purim, when it is called "bread of Mordecai."

Marzipan was and still is a luxury. Since it's very difficult to make the pure almond paste, or "base paste," at home, most candymakers buy the paste and mix it with powdered sugar and other ingredients to get the right taste and texture. Because of its expense and the fact that it is not generally available, except at specialty stores, ways have been devised to concoct a make-believe marzipan that has the almond flavor and much the same texture but not the same price tag.

Cereal Marzipan

This recipe is nutritious and tastes great, but it does not lend itself well to modeling little figures. Since the mixture is rather dark, it is best suited to shaping "potatoes" and rolling the balls in cinnamon or cocoa.

You will need a measuring cup and spoons, mixing bowl, fork, saucer, and:

    ½ cup wheat germ *or* ½ cup oatmeal whirled fine in a blender
    1½ tablespoons sugar
    2 tablespoons milk
    ½ teaspoon almond flavoring
    1½ tablespoons soft butter or margarine
    2 tablespoons cinnamon *or* 2 tablespoons cocoa powder
    1 tablespoon powdered sugar

Put the wheat germ or oatmeal, sugar, milk, almond flavoring, and butter or margarine in a bowl and mix well. Knead with your hands to make a smooth, heavy paste.

Form the paste into one-inch balls. Mix the cinnamon or cocoa powder with the powdered sugar in a saucer. Roll the balls in the mixture. Toss them lightly to shake off the excess. Use a toothpick to put "eyes" in the potato if you wish. The butter or margarine in the recipe will soak through the cinnamon or cocoa mix and darken it.

Cover and keep in the refrigerator. This recipe makes about two dozen balls.

Potato Marzipan Potatoes

You will need a small saucepan, potholder, fork, knife, measuring cup and spoons, mixing bowl, wax paper, saucer and:

> 1 small potato
> lightly salted water
> 1½ cups powdered sugar, without lumps (If lumpy, crush with a spoon.)
> 1 teaspoon almond flavoring
> 2 tablespoons graham cracker crumbs *or* 2 tablespoons wheat germ
> 2 tablespoons cinnamon *or* 2 tablespoons cocoa powder
> 1 tablespoon powdered sugar

Boil the potato in a saucepan with enough salted water to half cover it. After about twenty minutes stab the potato with a fork or the tip of a sharp knife to see if it is tender.

Cool the potato under cold running water until you can handle it. Use the knife or your fingers to peel off the skin. Mash the potato thoroughly on a piece of wax paper and place two tablespoons of it in a mixing bowl. You will not need the leftover potato, unless you want to make another batch.

Slowly add 1½ cups of powdered sugar, a little at a time, blending it with the fork. The potato will gradually dissolve the sugar and form a creamy paste. Add enough sugar to make a stiff dough, like clay. Add the almond flavoring and work in the graham cracker crumbs or wheat germ.

Form the dough into one-inch balls. Mix the cinnamon or cocoa powder with the one tablespoon of powdered sugar in a saucer. Roll the balls in the mixture. Toss them lightly to shake off the excess. Use a toothpick to put "eyes" in the potato if you wish.

Cover and keep in the refrigerator. This recipe makes about two dozen balls.

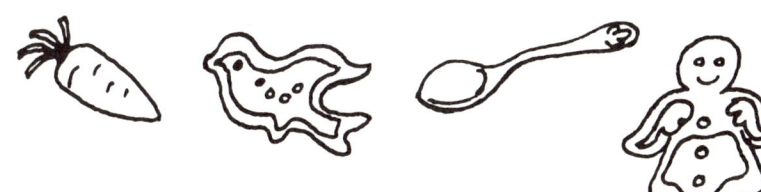

Potato Marzipan Miniatures

Follow the recipe on page 24 for Potato Marzipan Potatoes *except* omit the graham cracker crumbs or wheat germ and the cinnamon or cocoa powder mix. You will also need a spoon and an artist's brush and food coloring.

Shape the marzipan into tiny people or animals or miniature fruits or vegetables or other figures. Paint them with food coloring. You can use it straight from the bottle, or when you need less brilliant shades, squeeze a few drops in the bowl of a spoon and add a couple of drops of water.

One easy shape is a fried egg: a flat circle with a smaller, slightly rounded circle on top of it, the whole thing no more than an inch across. Paint the yolk of the egg with bright yellow.

Don't be afraid to experiment. Even the mistakes are edible. Let the figures dry. Then cover them tightly and keep them in the refrigerator.

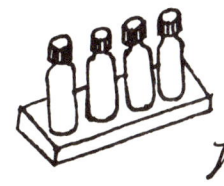
food color set

Inevitably different countries developed different kinds of candy to suit different tastes. France made crystallized fruits and sugared almonds. Italy had small hard candies called *confetti*. Walnuts mixed with a sweet sugar paste were popular in several countries. Meanwhile, in the American colonies, early settlers used maple syrup and maple sugar. The Dutch bakers in New Amsterdam were among the first commercial candymakers in the colonies.

England was the first to manufacture hard candies on a large scale, beginning in the nineteenth century. But it remained for the United States and modern technology to put candymaking among the leading food industries of the twentieth century.

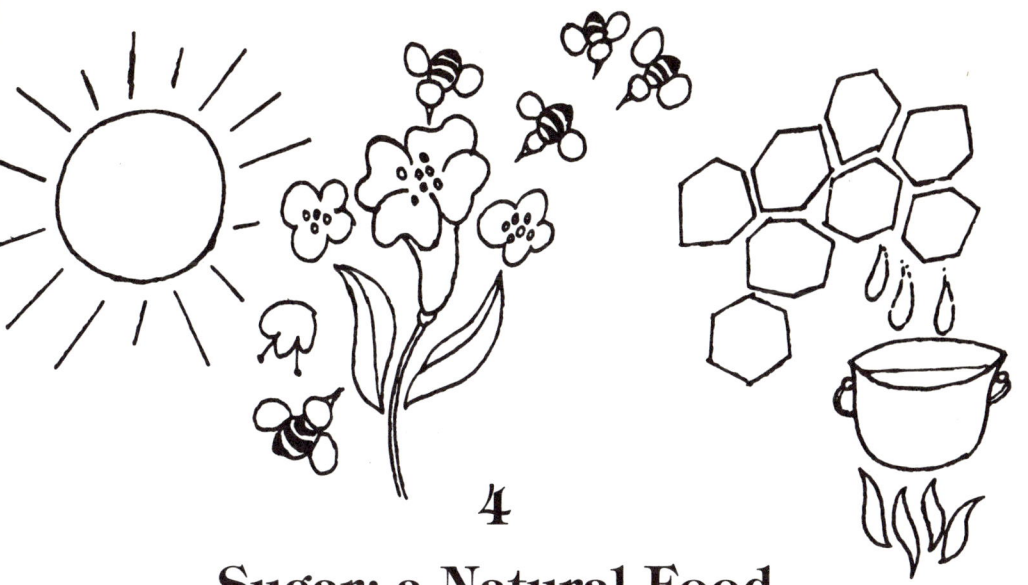

4

Sugar: a Natural Food

Nobody quite understands why it is that sweet things taste so good, although much is known about the chemistry of sweets. Many things are naturally sweet-tasting—fruit, for example, and the sap of certain kinds of trees and the juice of some plants like the sugar cane and sugar beet. By a process called photosynthesis, sunlight acts on chlorophyll, the green substance in the plant leaves, causing carbon dioxide to combine chemically with water to form sucrose, a kind of sugar. Sucrose, which can be broken down chemically into two other sugars—glucose and fructose—is carried from the leaves to other parts of the plant and stored there. Fruit tastes sweet because of the fructose stored in the fleshy part of the fruit to nourish its seeds. The bee carries sweet nectar, containing fructose, from the flower and puts it in one of the wax cells of the honeycomb. As water evaporates, the nectar thickens and becomes honey. The juice of the sugar cane and the sap from certain trees, such as the sugar maple, is boiled to evaporate the water and produce thicker, sweeter syrup. In the nineteenth century it was discovered that the juice of the sugar beet is an excellent sweetener. Sugar from sugar beets is identical to cane sugar. Although the beet is cultivated in cooler climates than the sugar cane can tolerate, the yield per acre is less and the cost of refining is higher.

Sugar is a pure chemical substance that crystallizes from the juice of the cane as it is boiled, leaving behind molasses syrup. Light molasses has a high sugar content, but as more and more sugar is crystallized from it, the remaining molasses becomes darker, more concentrated, and less sweet. So-called blackstrap molasses has the least sugar, but it does contain a high percentage of calcium and some iron.

Sugar, chemically pure sucrose, is a carbohydrate. It offers readily available food energy, but it does not build or repair vital body tissue. For this reason foods with high sugar content are often condemned by nutrition experts as "empty calories" that take the place of important body-builders in the diet. Sugar has sometimes even been made to seem a villain, poisoning the systems of the human body, not merely replacing other foods.

But there is disagreement among the nutritionists. Some who condemn sugar say honey is much better for you; others insist that honey is harmful, too. Still another group says if you must use sugar, then use raw sugar. But true "raw" sugar is not fit to eat because it contains many impurities. What the raw-sugar advocates mean is turbinado, light brown crystals still coated with molasses that has not been completely removed by refining. Regular brown sugar is refined sugar to which molasses has been added. It would seem that there is little difference in nutritional value; the main difference is in price. Odd as it seems, less refined foods are often more expensive than more refined foods for which there is a greater demand.

The carbohydrate of honey is for chemical reasons more readily used by the body than the more complex sugar crystals. But the slight amounts of minerals it contains are not enough to make it superior to sugar. Whether sugar is granulated white, brown, or "raw" and sold at higher prices, it is still simply pure carbohydrate.

In the days of prehistoric man, and in fact until this century, there was little danger of anyone's eating too many sweets. They were just too expensive. But in recent years sugar has come to be thought of as an inexpensive source of quick energy, something important to soldiers and sometimes to athletes, but not essential for most people, who get all the carbohydrates they need from a diet that includes fruits, vegetables, and cereals. Nobody *needs* sugar, although most people enjoy it in some form.

There is no doubt sugar is harmful to the teeth. Queen Elizabeth I of England had rotten teeth, which have been blamed on her habit of eating sweets all day long. And studies show that tooth decay is more common in countries where a lot of sugar

is eaten than in places where civilization has not brought soft-drink and candy machines.

Most experts agree that it is not sugar in the *diet* that is to be blamed so much as it is sugar in the *mouth*. The bacteria that attack teeth thrive in carbohydrates that stick to the teeth and lodge in the crevices. Continually sipping soft drinks or eating candy that stays in contact with the teeth may help cause decay.

The solution, then, is to brush your teeth regularly and thoroughly. But that isn't all: proper diet that includes a lot of calcium for building strong bones and teeth is also necessary. It also helps to inherit a tendency to strong, healthy teeth from your parents and grandparents.

If you eat right and brush right, you can enjoy candy in moderation.

Here are some candies that were made long before candymaking became the big business that it is today. In addition to sugar, they're made with nutritious ingredients that include cereals, fruit, and nuts.

Molasses-Coconut Candy

On the islands where sugar cane is cultivated and coconut palms grow, sugar and coconut are combined to make a simple and wholesome candy with a strong molasses flavor and a chewy texture.

You will need a measuring cup, 1½-quart saucepan, potholder, wooden mixing spoon, heat-proof plate, knife, wax paper, and:

    1 cup grated unsweetened coconut
        (available at health-food stores, or grate your own fresh coconut; see page 79 for opening the coconut)
    1 cup molasses
    butter or margarine

Put the coconut and molasses in the saucepan and cook over medium heat, stirring occasionally at first and then constantly as the mixture thickens. As it becomes thicker, turn the heat to low.

After about ten minutes of cooking, when the mixture is very thick and comes away from the sides of the pan, take it off the heat.

Grease a heat-proof plate with butter or margarine, and pour the molasses mixture on the plate.

After it has cooled, cut the candy in squares and wrap them in pieces of wax paper. There will be about three dozen one-inch squares.

 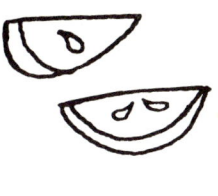  

Candied Apple Slices

Make these when the weather is quite dry.

You will need a measuring cup, small saucepan or skillet, potholder, slotted spoon, sharp knife, large wire rack, wax paper, brown paper bag, and:

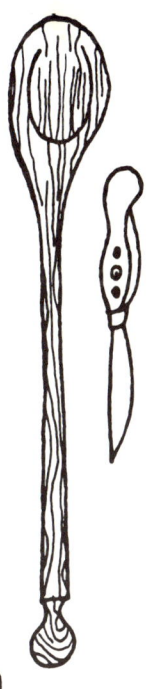

    4 medium-size apples
    1 cup sugar
    ½ cup water
    additional sugar
    additional water

Wash the apples, cut them into quarters, cut out the core, and peel them. Cut each quarter into three slices.

Put one cup of sugar and half a cup of water in a saucepan or skillet. Stir to dissolve the sugar and bring the mixture to a boil. Use the slotted spoon to lower twelve apple slices into the boiling syrup. Cook for about five minutes, until the apples look woolly and the edges are beginning to look translucent.

Lift the slices out of the syrup with the slotted spoon and place them on the wire rack over a sheet of wax paper to catch the drips.

Add ¼ cup of water to the syrup to replace the water that has boiled away. Cook twelve more slices. Always add an additional ¼ cup of water after each batch.

Put the rack of apple slices in a dry place overnight. The next day, put ½ cup of sugar in a small paper bag and drop in about six of the sticky apple slices. Squeeze shut the top of the bag and shake it. Lay each sugared apple slice on the rack. Sugar all the slices, a few at a time, adding more sugar to the bag as it is used up. Save any that is left over or that falls under the rack.

Let the sugar slices dry on the rack overnight. The next day, put more sugar in the paper bag and shake them all again. Let them dry one more day. By this time they should be firm and dry. If they are still sticky and oozing, let them dry a little longer. Store them in flat layers separated by sheets of wax paper. There will be forty-eight slices.

Sugarplums

Sugarplums were originally made in Portugal, where fruits were cooked slowly in heavy sugar syrups until they became glazed. Here is a much simpler recipe that requires no cooking at all. Instead, dried fruits are stuffed with a sweet filling and rolled in sugar.

You will need a small sharp knife, saucer, wax paper, and:

Sugar: a Natural Food

> 1 batch of Honey Balls (page 14), Cereal Marzipan (page 23), Potato Marzipan (page 24), or Cream Cheese Filling (below)
> 2 dozen dried dates, prunes, or figs
> ½ cup powdered sugar

First, make any one of the fillings listed above. Form twenty-four balls, but do not roll them in a coating. Set them aside.

Slit each piece of fruit along one side with a knife, making a pocket. Place one ball in each pocket, shaping it to fit.

Roll the stuffed fruit in powdered sugar in a saucer and place on wax paper until dry.

This recipe makes two dozen Sugarplums. Store them covered in the refrigerator.

Cream Cheese Filling

You will need a measuring cup and spoons, mixing bowl, fork, and:

> 2 tablespoons cream cheese
> 2 tablespoons milk
> 2 cups powdered sugar, without lumps
> ½ teaspoon vanilla

Put the cream cheese in a bowl and let it soften at room temperature for half an hour. Stir in the milk a little at a time.

Gradually add just enough powdered sugar to make a firm dough. Add the vanilla.

Mix the batch thoroughly and knead it with your hands.

Honey Popcorn Balls

You will need a popcorn popper or large heavy pot with a lid, measuring cup, large mixing bowl, deep saucepan, potholder, candy thermometer, wooden mixing spoon, fork, and:

    3 tablespoons cooking oil
    ½ cup unpopped popcorn
    ⅔ cup sugar
    ⅔ cup honey
      butter or margarine

Follow the directions for the popcorn popper. Or put the oil in a pot and heat it until two or three test kernels of corn will pop. Add the rest of the popcorn. There should be no more than one layer of popcorn on the bottom of the pot. If the pot is not large enough, make the popcorn in two batches.

Put on the lid, turn the heat to medium, and shake the pot or tip it back and forth to keep the kernels moving so they don't burn before they are popped. When all the popping has stopped, remove the lid.

Place the popcorn in a large mixing bowl. You will have about eight cups; a little more or less won't matter. Be sure to pick out any unpopped kernels or hulls.

Put the sugar and honey in a saucepan. Heat them, stirring, until the sugar is dissolved and the mixture starts to boil. Put the candy thermometer into the mixture and cook to 245 degrees.

Pour the honey syrup over the popcorn in a thin stream, stirring with a fork while you pour. Keep tossing the popcorn to coat it evenly.

When it has cooled enough to handle but has not yet hardened, rub a little butter or margarine on the palms of your hands. Then form the popcorn into balls, squeezing it gently to make the popcorn stick together.

This recipe will make about sixteen balls the size of snowballs. Store them in a plastic bag after they are cool.

Sugar Popcorn Balls

You will need a popcorn popper or large heavy pot with a lid, measuring cups and spoons, a large mixing bowl, 1½-quart saucepan, potholder, candy thermometer, wooden mixing spoon, fork, and:

    3 tablespoons cooking oil
    ½ cup unpopped popcorn
    1 cup sugar
    ⅓ cup light corn syrup
    ⅓ cup water
    3 tablespoons butter or margarine
    ½ teaspoon salt
    1 teaspoon vanilla
      additional butter or margarine

Pop the popcorn, following the directions given in the Honey Popcorn Balls recipe on page 36.

Put the sugar, corn syrup, water, butter or margarine, and salt in a saucepan. Stir until the sugar is dissolved and the mixture starts to boil. Put the candy thermometer into the mixture and cook without stirring to 250 degrees. This will take only a few minutes. Remove from the heat and stir in the vanilla.

Pour the sugar syrup over the popcorn in a thin stream, stirring with a fork while you pour. Keep tossing the popcorn to coat it evenly.

Follow the directions in Honey Popcorn Balls for making the balls and storing them. This recipe will make about sixteen balls.

Caramel Popcorn

Caramel Popcorn tastes much like Cracker Jack, the candy-coated popcorn with a toy in every box. But it requires extra special care to make. One step produces steam that can burn you, so be *very* careful.

You will need a popcorn popper or large heavy pot with a lid, measuring cups, a large mixing bowl,

Sugar: a Natural Food

small saucepan, potholder, candy thermometer, wooden spoon, fork, wax paper, and:

> 3 tablespoons cooking oil
> ½ cup unpopped popcorn
> ⅔ cup sugar
> ½ cup hot water
> ⅓ cup brown sugar, firmly packed
> ½ cup salted peanuts, if desired

Pop the popcorn, following the directions in the Honey Popcorn Balls recipe on page 36.

Put the sugar—only the sugar—in a saucepan and turn on the heat to medium. Stir it constantly with a wooden spoon. The sugar will melt, gradually at first, then faster and faster, turning a deep golden brown. When it is melted and brown, remove it from the heat. This is called caramelized sugar.

VERY CAREFULLY pour the hot water into the caramelized sugar. It will make a big cloud of steam, which can burn you. Do not stand with your face or hands close to the saucepan.

When the steam settles down, add the brown sugar. Put the saucepan back on the heat and stir the mixture with a spoon until it begins to boil. Put in the candy thermometer and cook without stirring to 238 degrees.

Pour the caramel syrup over the popcorn in a thin stream, stirring with a fork while you pour. Keep tossing the popcorn to coat it evenly. Add salted peanuts, if you want them.

When the popcorn is completely coated, spread it out on a sheet of wax paper to cool and harden. When it is no longer sticky, store it in a plastic bag.

Brown Sugar Popcorn Balls

This recipe is easier to make than Caramel Popcorn, but the taste is similar.

You will need a popcorn popper or large heavy pot with a lid, measuring cups and spoons, large mixing bowl, deep saucepan, potholder, candy thermometer, wooden mixing spoon, fork, wax paper, and:

- 3 tablespoons cooking oil
- ½ cup unpopped popcorn
- 2 cups brown sugar, firmly packed
- 1 cup water
- 2 tablespoons vinegar
- 4 tablespoons butter or margarine
- additional butter or margarine

Pop the popcorn, following the directions in the Honey Popcorn Balls recipe on page 36.

Put the sugar, water, and vinegar in a small saucepan, bring the mixture to a boil, and cook it for ten minutes.

Add the butter or margarine. When it has melted, put the candy thermometer into the mixture and cook without stirring to 260 degrees. This takes only a few minutes.

Pour the brown sugar syrup over the popcorn in a thin stream, stirring with a fork while you pour. Keep tossing the popcorn to coat it evenly.

Follow the directions in the Honey Popcorn Balls recipe on page 36 for making the balls and storing them. This recipe makes about sixteen balls.

Candied Cereals

Recipes for candied popcorn can be used to make candied cereal. Any fairly small-grained cold cereal is suitable: puffed wheat, puffed rice, rice cereal, or even cornflake-type cereals may be used. Here are some possible variations:

For added nutrition, use one of the high-protein cereals.

Use a combination of cereals, such as half puffed rice and half cornflakes.

Mix the cereals with popcorn.

Add sesame seeds or sunflower seeds.

Add salted peanuts.

Add grated coconut.

5

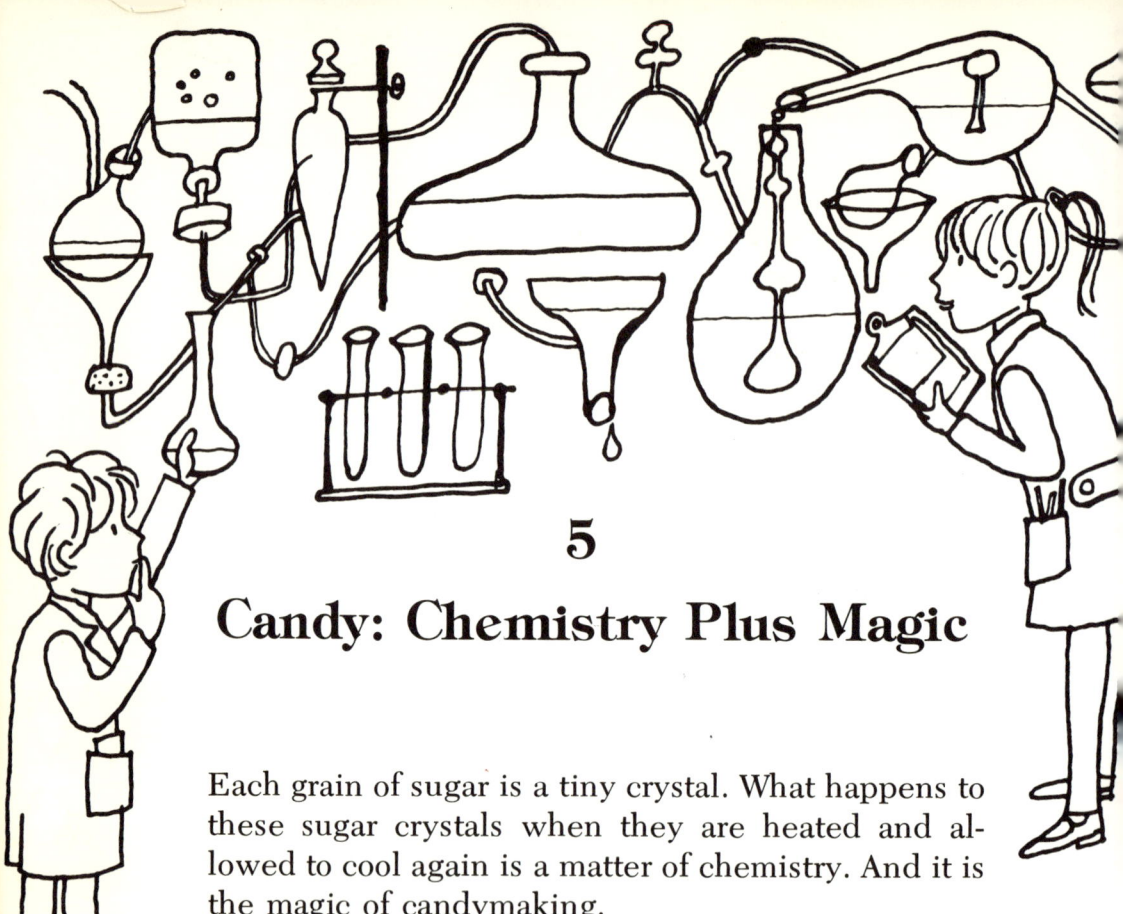

Candy: Chemistry Plus Magic

Each grain of sugar is a tiny crystal. What happens to these sugar crystals when they are heated and allowed to cool again is a matter of chemistry. And it is the magic of candymaking.

The simplest candy is a mixture of sugar and water. Flavorings and other ingredients affect the way the candy tastes. But the most important change is the way the sugar crystallizes as it cools. In most cooked candy, the crystals of sugar are dissolved in water or liquid that contains water. When the syrup is cooked, some of the water boils away, and the syrup becomes more concentrated. The temperature it reaches determines how much water remains in the syrup. The amount of water in the syrup and the way the syrup is handled as it cools determines the size of the crystals that will be formed again. Candymakers call this characteristic the *grain*. It's the grain, together with the firmness, that tells you what kind of candy it is.

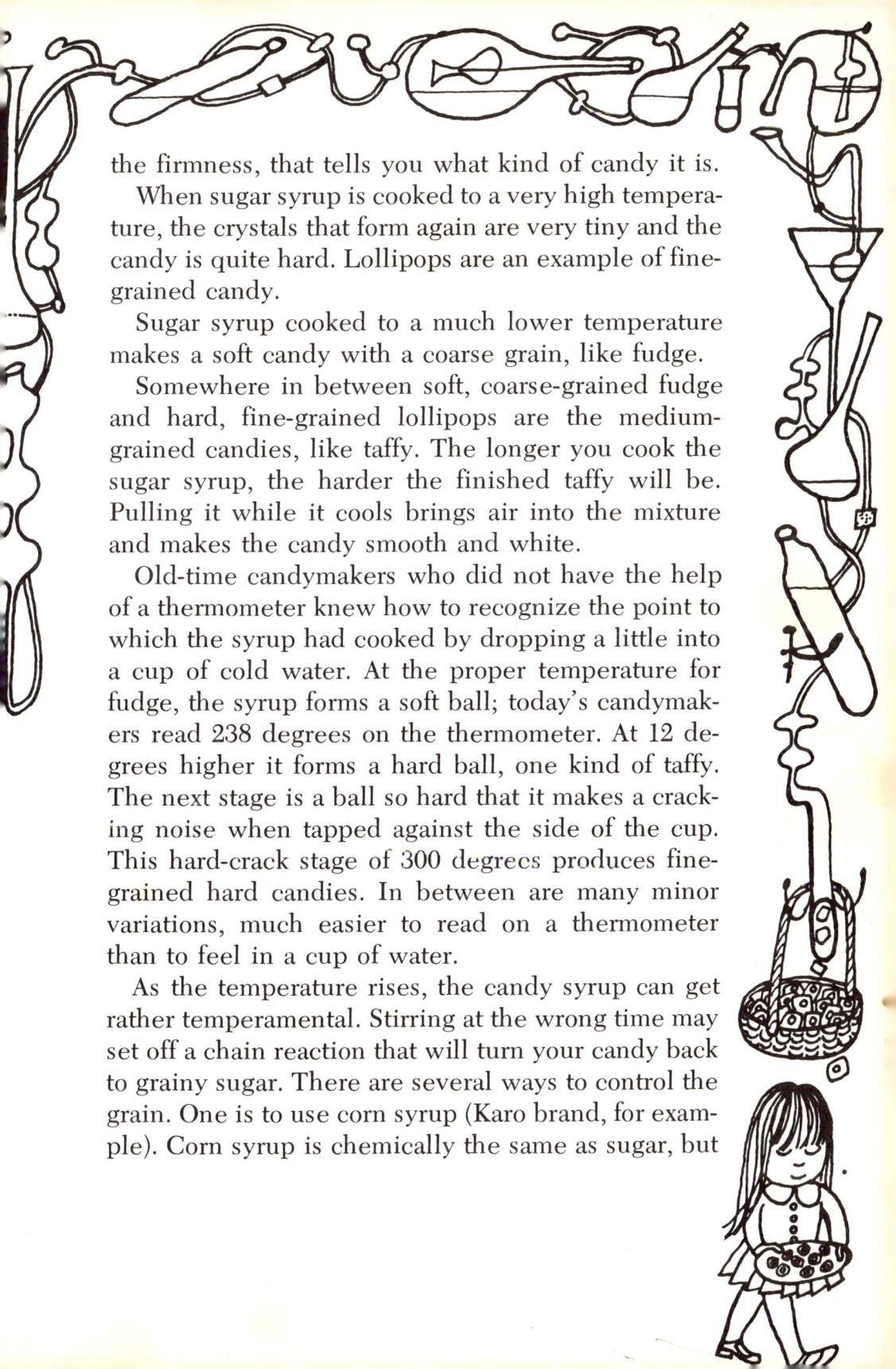

When sugar syrup is cooked to a very high temperature, the crystals that form again are very tiny and the candy is quite hard. Lollipops are an example of fine-grained candy.

Sugar syrup cooked to a much lower temperature makes a soft candy with a coarse grain, like fudge.

Somewhere in between soft, coarse-grained fudge and hard, fine-grained lollipops are the medium-grained candies, like taffy. The longer you cook the sugar syrup, the harder the finished taffy will be. Pulling it while it cools brings air into the mixture and makes the candy smooth and white.

Old-time candymakers who did not have the help of a thermometer knew how to recognize the point to which the syrup had cooked by dropping a little into a cup of cold water. At the proper temperature for fudge, the syrup forms a soft ball; today's candymakers read 238 degrees on the thermometer. At 12 degrees higher it forms a hard ball, one kind of taffy. The next stage is a ball so hard that it makes a cracking noise when tapped against the side of the cup. This hard-crack stage of 300 degrees produces fine-grained hard candies. In between are many minor variations, much easier to read on a thermometer than to feel in a cup of water.

As the temperature rises, the candy syrup can get rather temperamental. Stirring at the wrong time may set off a chain reaction that will turn your candy back to grainy sugar. There are several ways to control the grain. One is to use corn syrup (Karo brand, for example). Corn syrup is chemically the same as sugar, but it does not crystallize and it helps to keep the sugar from recrystallizing at the wrong time. Most candy recipes call for some corn syrup. Other recipes use an acid, like lemon juice or vinegar, or a neutralizer, like cream of tartar or bicarbonate of soda, as a way of controlling the grain in candy.

Knowing when to stir and when not to stir is important. As a general rule, stir the ingredients gently to mix them, but do not stir after the syrup boils (unless the recipe specifically tells you to stir). Fudge and other coarse-grained candies are beaten as they cool to introduce air into the mixture while the sugar recrystallizes. Air makes it light and creamy. Taffy is pulled for the same reason. But hard candy is not stirred at all; you want as few air bubbles in it as possible.

Clear Candy Circles

Cooked to a high temperature, hard candy is easy to make because it does not require any special handling, like beating or pulling. The simplest clear candy to make is a plain circle. If you have lollipop sticks, add them to the circles to make lollipops. And if you have miniature molds, you can pour syrup into them to make interesting shapes, like the old fashioned "clear toys."

You will need measuring cups and spoons, a saucepan, potholder, wooden mixing spoon, candy thermometer, two baking sheets, teaspoon, paper towels, plastic wrap, and:

Candy: Chemistry Plus Magic

    1 cup sugar
    ½ cup water
    ⅓ cup light corn syrup
       vegetable or mineral oil
    1 teaspoon orange or lemon flavoring
       food coloring
       additional sugar

Put the sugar, water, and corn syrup in the saucepan. Heat them, stirring, until the sugar is dissolved and the mixture starts to boil. Put the candy thermometer into the mixture and cook to 300 degrees.

Take the saucepan off the heat and let the syrup cool until it stops bubbling. While it cools, grease the baking sheets or several miniature molds with oil.

Very gently stir flavoring and several drops of food coloring into the candy syrup. Drop pools of syrup onto the baking sheets from a teaspoon, making the pools far enough apart so they don't run together. (Or pour the syrup into the molds or over the ends of lollipop sticks.) If the syrup gets too thick before you have finished, reheat it slightly.

After a few minutes, when the candies have hardened and cooled, lift them off the baking sheet and lay them on a paper towel to absorb the oil.

To keep the candies from sticking together, wrap them separately in pieces of plastic wrap. Or dampen them between layers of wet paper towels and dust them with granulated sugar; this is called "sanding." Set them aside to dry thoroughly before storing in a tight-lidded can or jar. This recipe makes about three dozen one-inch candies.

Vanilla Cream Fudge

There are many different ways to make and flavor fudge, and they are all delicious. This kind is sometimes called Opera Fudge.

You will need measuring cups and spoons, a deep saucepan, potholder, wooden mixing spoon, candy thermometer, pie pan or deep plate, knife, and:

- 2 cups sugar
- 1½ cups Half-and-Half *or* mixture of milk and cream
- 2 tablespoons light corn syrup
- 1 teaspoon vanilla
- butter or margarine
- ½ cup chopped nuts, if desired

Put the sugar, Half-and-Half, and corn syrup in a saucepan. Heat them, stirring, until the sugar is dissolved and the mixture starts to boil. Put the candy thermometer into the mixture and cook slowly to 238 degrees. This may take a long time—about forty-five minutes.

Take the saucepan off the heat and let it cool until the bottom of the pan feels comfortably warm. Stir in the vanilla.

Lightly grease a pie pan or plate with butter or margarine. Beat the candy syrup as hard as you can. It will be very stiff. After a few minutes the candy will look lighter in color and less shiny. Stir in the nuts, if you want them.

Spread the fudge in the pan and let it set until it is quite firm. Before it hardens completely, dip a knife into hot water, wipe the water off the blade, and cut the fudge into three dozen squares.

Penuche

Pronounced *peNOOchee* and sometimes called by its Mexican Spanish name of *panocha*, meaning "little bread," this fudge is made with brown sugar instead of white. Otherwise, it is made the same way as Vanilla Cream Fudge.

You will need the same equipment as for Vanilla Cream Fudge and:

    1 one-pound box light brown sugar
    ¾ cup milk
    1 teaspoon vanilla
        butter or margarine
    ½ cup chopped nuts, if desired

Put the brown sugar and milk in a saucepan and follow the directions for the Vanilla Cream Fudge recipe on page 46.

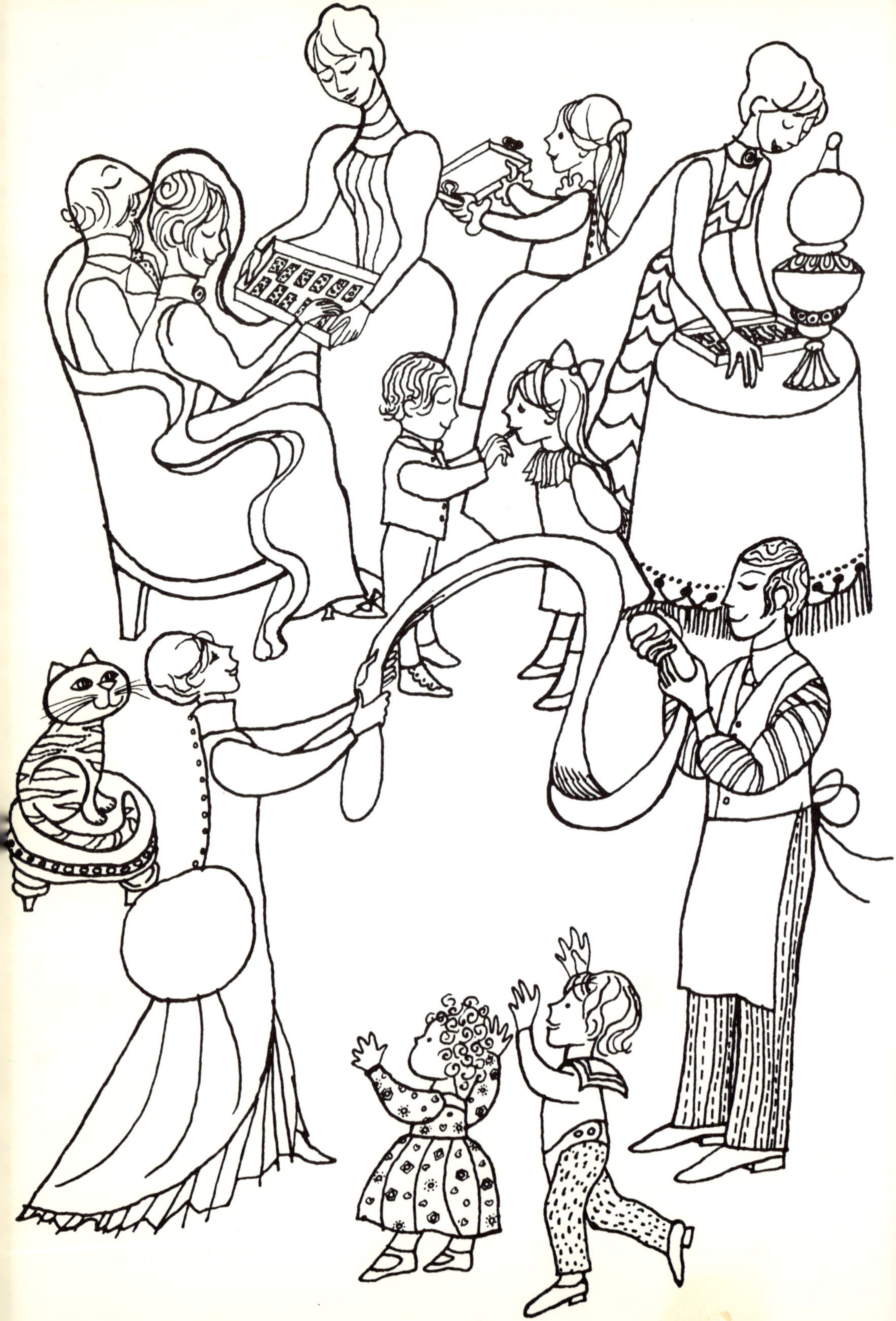

6

Old-fashioned Favorites

Once upon a time, when your great-grandmothers were young, taffy pulls were gay social events. Even today, pulling taffy seems to be more fun when there are other people around to help. Salt water taffy, said to have been made originally with sea water, is sold along the boardwalks of Atlantic City and other New Jersey seashore towns where passersby can watch mechanical taffy pullers tirelessly at work.

There are lots of different recipes for taffy, and everyone seems to have a favorite. In some recipes, the syrup is cooked to a fairly high temperature, which results in a rather hard taffy that is easier to handle when you are pulling it. Taffy cooked to a low temperature is soft and chewy but much harder to handle.

To keep the taffy from sticking to your hands, coat your hands with butter or powdered sugar or cornstarch. Keep a supply handy so that you can coat your hands again when necessary. But try to use as little as possible. You can also do what the professionals do and wear clean cotton gloves—not dress gloves but non-fuzzy work gloves.

Taffy is *hygroscopic,* which means that it absorbs moisture from the air and becomes sticky unless it has been tightly wrapped. Before you begin, cut about three dozen two-inch squares of wax paper or plastic wrap.

Taffy

You will need measuring cups and spoons, a saucepan, potholder, wooden mixing spoon, candy thermometer, large platter or baking sheet, scissors or knife, and:

    1 cup sugar
    ¼ cup water
    ¼ cup light corn syrup
    1 teaspoon vinegar
    1 teaspoon butter or margarine
    ½ teaspoon salt
      additional butter or margarine
    1 teaspoon vanilla
      cornstarch or powdered sugar

Put the sugar, water, corn syrup, vinegar, butter or margarine, and salt in the saucepan. Heat them, stirring, until the mixture starts to boil. Put in the candy thermometer and cook to 250 degrees for *soft taffy* or to 265 degrees for *hard taffy.*

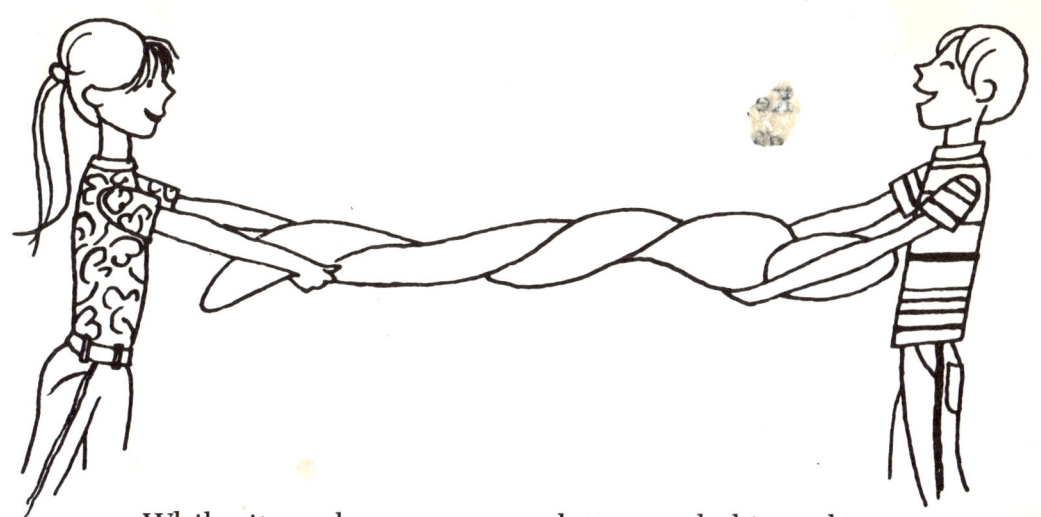

While it cooks, grease a platter or baking sheet with butter or margarine. Then pour the cooked syrup onto the platter. Let it cool for about five minutes. Sprinkle the vanilla over the cooling syrup, which has begun to set, and pull the edges of the mass of candy over the center, covering the vanilla.

While the candy is still quite warm (but not hot—it will burn you), coat your hands and begin to pull the soft, sticky mass. Pull it into a rope about two feet long; fold the rope in half, twist it, and pull it again. Keep pulling, folding, and twisting until the candy is white, smooth, and satiny and is beginning to feel firm. Stop pulling while it is still warm and somewhat soft. If you pull too long, the candy will get too hard.

Starting at one end, pull and twist the taffy into a rope about ½ inch thick. Dip scissors or a knife in powdered sugar or cornstarch and, as you pull, cut the rope into pieces about 1½ inches long. Wrap each piece individually in wax paper or plastic wrap and twist the ends tightly. You'll have about three dozen pieces.

Marshmallows

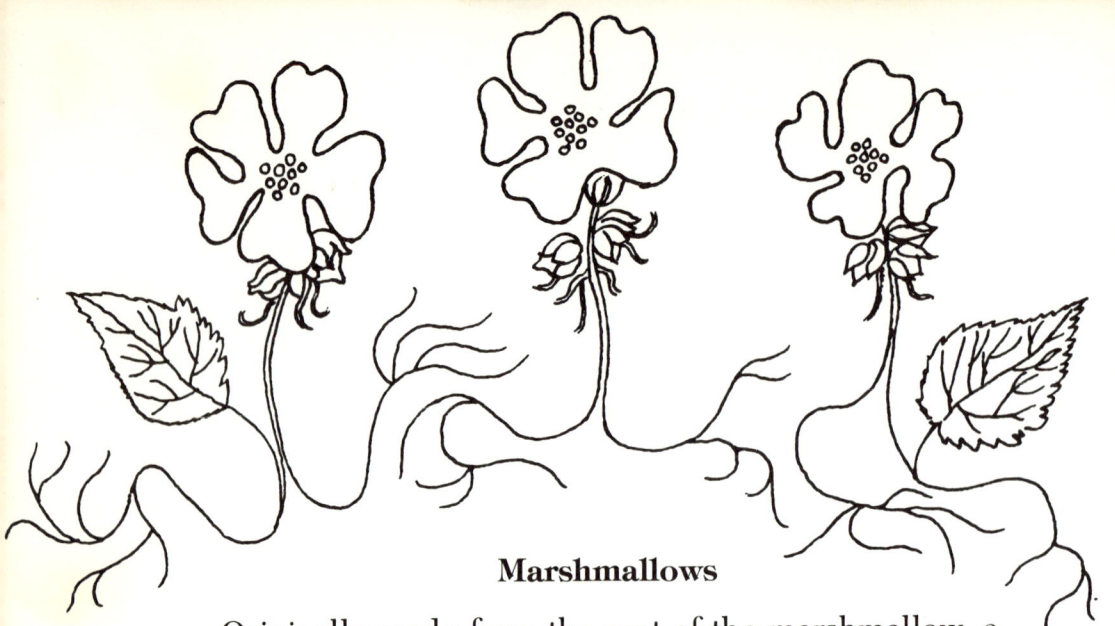

Originally made from the root of the marshmallow, a pink-flowered plant that grows wild in marshes and was once used as a medicine for sore throats and coughs, marshmallow is a coarse-grained candy like fudge. Gelatin changes the texture of the candy, and long beating is important to make it light and fluffy and to help it keep its shape.

You will need a baking sheet, measuring cups and spoons, a mixing bowl, saucepan, wooden mixing spoon, potholder, candy thermometer, electric mixer, 8-inch-square cake pan, wax paper, knife, and:

  1 cup shredded coconut
    or powdered sugar
  butter or margarine
  cornstarch
  1 package unflavored gelatin
  ¼ cup cold water
  1 cup sugar
  ¼ cup water
  ⅓ cup light corn syrup
  1 teaspoon vanilla

Old-fashioned Favorites

If you want to coat the marshmallows in coconut, spread the coconut evenly on a baking sheet and toast in an oven preheated to 350 degrees. After three minutes, stir the coconut so that it toasts evenly. Watch it closely so that it doesn't get too dark. When it is golden brown, take it out of the oven and let it cool.

Grease the cake pan with butter or margarine. Dust it evenly with cornstarch. Sprinkle 1/3 cup of toasted coconut, if you are using it, over the bottom of the pan.

Put the gelatin in a mixing bowl and add 1/4 cup cold water. Stir it and set it aside to soften.

Put the sugar, 1/4 cup water, and corn syrup in the saucepan. Heat them, stirring, until the mixture starts to boil. Put the candy thermometer into the mixture and cook to 244 degrees.

Pour the candy syrup slowly into the softened gelatin and beat the mixture with the electric mixer until it is very thick and the peaks hold their shape when you raise the beater. It will take about fifteen minutes of steady beating. The mixture will still be warm. Stir in the vanilla. Pour the mixture into the prepared pan.

When it has cooled completely, cut the marshmallow into thirty-six squares with a sharp knife dipped in powdered sugar or cornstarch. Spread the rest of the toasted coconut or a few spoons of powdered sugar on a piece of wax paper. Loosen the marshmallow squares, remove them from the pan, and roll them in the coating.

Put the marshmallows on a plate and cover them with plastic wrap.

Easy Fondant Patties

Fondant is one of the simplest forms of candy. It is the soft cream filling that is used inside dipped chocolates, and it is the basis for other candies as well. In true fondant, the sugar and water syrup is cooked like fudge, poured out on a clean surface (marble slabs were once used for this and other kinds of candymaking), and worked by gathering the cooling mixture together and spreading it out again with a spatula. As this creaming goes on, the mixture becomes white and firm, until it is stiff enough to be molded and used as a filling or mixed with other ingredients.

True fondant is creamy and smooth and softer than fudge, and it is quite tricky to make. Many candy cooks use simpler ways to make a good-tasting fondant that does not take so much time and skill.

You will need a measuring cup and spoons, mixing bowl, fork, wax paper, and:

    1 egg white
    2 cups powdered sugar, without lumps
    2 teaspoons soft butter or margarine
    ½ teaspoon vanilla, peppermint, or other flavoring
    food coloring, if desired

Separate the egg white from the yolk and put it in the mixing bowl. Store the egg yolk in a covered jar with a little cold water and use it in scrambled eggs or another recipe.

Beat the egg white with a fork until it is foamy. Gradually stir in the powdered sugar. Add the butter

Old-fashioned Favorites

or margarine, flavoring, and a few drops of food coloring if you wish.

Mix the batch thoroughly and knead it with your hands. Form the fondant into one-inch balls, set them on a sheet of wax paper, and flatten them into patties with the palms of your hands.

This recipe makes about twenty-four patties. Store them in a tightly lidded container to keep them from drying out.

Old-fashioned Rock Candy

Rock candy requires almost no effort on the part of the cook. It is made by cooking a sugar and water solution and letting the sugar recrystallize. The new crystals will be much larger than the original crystals. The more concentrated you make the syrup, the bigger the crystals will be.

You will need a measuring cup and spoon, saucepan, mixing spoon, glass jar, string, Popsicle or other stick, paper clip, and:

     1 cup sugar
     4 tablespoons water

Put the sugar and water in the saucepan. Heat, stirring, only until the sugar is completely dissolved.

Cut a piece of string two inches longer than the height of the jar. Tie one end around the stick. Tie the paper clip to the other end. Lay the stick across the top of the jar with the string suspended.

Pour the sugar solution into the jar and let it stand undisturbed for about two weeks while sugar crystals form around the string.

7

Xocolatl to Chocolate

It's hard to think about "candy" without thinking about "chocolate." But long before the first chocolate candy was made, the Aztec Indians of ancient Mexico had concocted a thick, bitter drink from the beans of the cacao tree.

Columbus, on one of his early voyages to the West Indies, had taken a few of these brown beans back to Ferdinand and Isabella, who regarded them as useless curiosities. But a few years later, in 1519, Cortez and his Spanish explorers were served a cold, frothy beverage called *xocolatl,* meaning "bitter water." Montezuma, the Aztec emperor, drank it from golden goblets, suitable to what the Aztecs regarded as its divine origin. The spelling was later changed to *chocolatl,* and the Spaniards, who did not like the drink as the Aztecs prepared it, found that adding sugar and spices and serving it hot made it much more to their taste.

Soon *chocolatl* was the most popular drink in the Spanish court. Cortez brought back not only a supply of cacao beans but also an understanding of how the cacao was cultivated and how the beans were prepared. Soon the evergreen cacao tree was growing in many Spanish possessions near the Equator, where the climate is hot and humid the year round. Chocolate (the spelling changed again) became a highly profitable industry for the Spanish, who managed for nearly a century to keep Cortez's information a secret from the rest of Europe. Then in 1615 some Spanish monks presented a wedding gift of chocolate to Louis XIII, the king of France. Soon the secret was out, and the popularity of chocolate spread to other countries. In 1657 the first English coffee house opened, where Londoners could gather to warm themselves with a hot drink and political discussion. Although still expensive, chocolate became so much in demand that Parliament added to the expense by levying a tax on every gallon made and sold.

Chocolate was beyond the reach of most people, high priced mainly because the cacao beans had to be ground by hand. Development of steam-driven grinders and other equipment speeded up the processing, and by 1730 the price had dropped to such a degree that it was within the grasp of nearly everyone. In 1765 the first chocolate factory in America was established in New England.

Still, chocolate was a *drink*. Then in 1875 in Switzerland, Daniel Peter invented a way to make milk chocolate that could be molded for eating as a candy. Today most chocolate is eaten, rather than drunk.

Although production methods have changed greatly, cacao is still grown as it was in the days of the Aztecs. About sixteen countries, all within twenty degrees of the Equator, produce cacao. South America was once the leading grower; now it is Africa. The tall, delicate evergreen trees produce leaves, flowers, and pods all at the same time, all year long. Expert pickers with long-handled knives lop the ripe pods from trunk and branches. The pods are gathered, and breakers crack them open with machetes. The beans are scooped out, cleaned, and allowed to ferment for several days. Then they are dried, sacked, and shipped to chocolate manufacturers.

One of the best-known chocolate companies in the country is a division of Hershey Foods, founded in 1900 by a man who disregarded all sensible advice and built his factory in the middle of farm country in south-central Pennsylvania. Today Hershey, Pennsylvania, is a major tourist attraction, where streets have been given names like Cocoa Avenue and streetlights are shaped like Hershey Kisses. The factory is one of the largest in the world, with about two million square feet of floor space.

In the Hershey factory, as in other chocolate factories, the beans are first roasted in revolving cylinders. Next a "cracker and fanner" removes the shells, leaving the meat of the beans, called the "nibs." The nibs, which contain more than half cocoa butter, are ground to a thick mass known as "chocolate liquor." With some of the cocoa butter removed, the liquor can be poured into molds to harden, forming cakes of bitter, unsweetened chocolate that is used in cooking and candymaking at home.

Cocoa (the spelling changed as well as the drink) is made by removing most of the cocoa butter and grinding the chocolate. (Cocoa butter has many uses, especially in soaps and cosmetics.) Eating chocolate is made by adding cocoa butter, along with sugar and sometimes milk, to the bitter chocolate to make a smooth paste. The paste is put in huge containers for *conching* (the *ch* is pronounced as in *church*): rollers knead the paste for long periods, sometimes for several days in the case of milk chocolate. (In the Her-

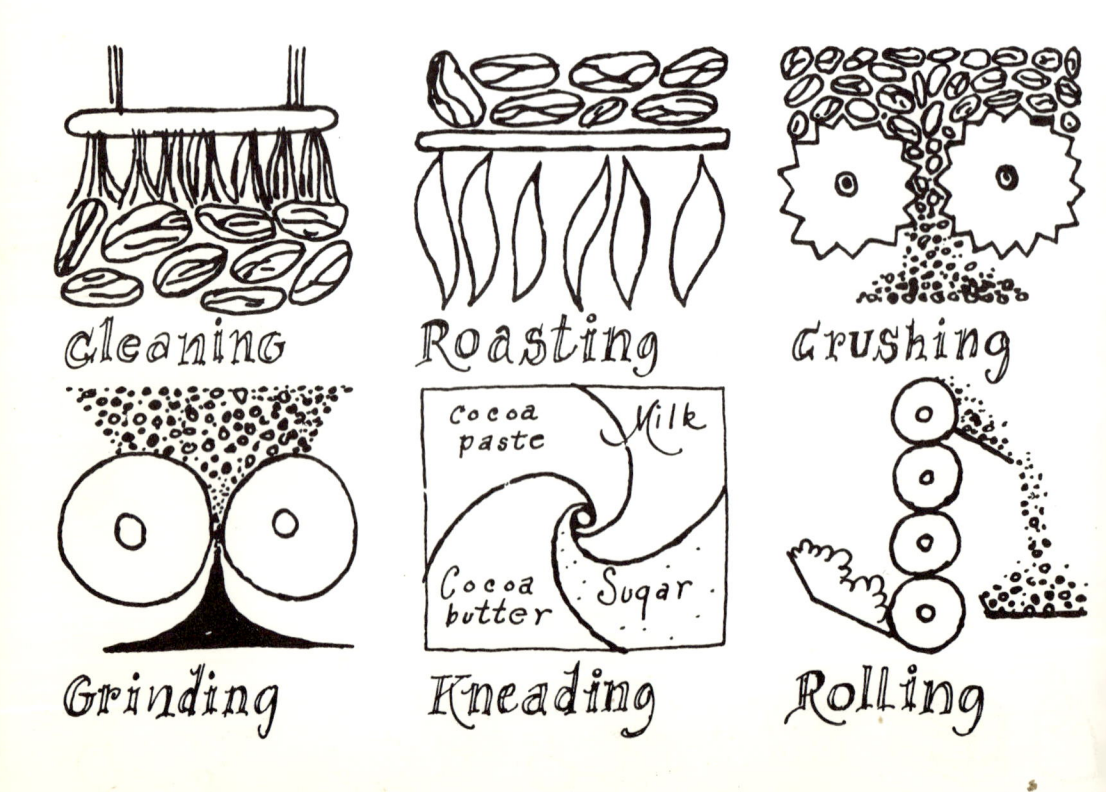

Cleaning   Roasting   Crushing

Grinding   Kneading   Rolling

Pressing — Cocoa Paste

Cocoa cake

Mold filling

Tapping, cooling

Demolding

Mold Filling

shey plant, one-third of the floor space is taken up by conches.) Finally, the smoothly textured chocolate is cast in molds to make candy bars, semisweet chocolate bits, and other candy shapes.

Fudge is one of the most popular homemade chocolate candies. It's not hard to make, and even if it doesn't turn out exactly as the recipe predicts, it's still good tasting. In the late 1800s, fudge was a favorite in women's colleges, like Vassar and Smith, where young ladies often broke "lights out" rules to cook the candy mixture over a gas lamp.

Here are recipes for six kinds of fudge. Some are made with cocoa, others with unsweetened chocolate, some with semisweet chocolate bits. Some use marshmallow topping; others call for brown sugar in addition to white. Some require rather long cooking, others are quick, and one takes no boiling at all.

None of these recipes lists nuts among the ingredients, but ½ cup or so of chopped nuts, added when you beat the fudge, are a delicious variation.

Probably the deciding factor in choosing a recipe will be whatever ingredients you have on hand. But eventually you'll want to try them all and find out which ones suit you best.

Chocolate Fudge I
(with unsweetened chocolate)

You will need measuring cups and spoons, a deep saucepan, potholder, wooden mixing spoon, candy thermometer, pie pan or deep plate, knife, and:

    2 one-ounce squares of unsweetened chocolate
    2 cups sugar
    ⅔ cup milk
    2 tablespoons light corn syrup
    1 tablespoon butter or margarine
    additional butter or margarine
    1 teaspoon vanilla

  Cut the squares of chocolate into small pieces. Put the sugar, milk, and corn syrup in the saucepan. Heat, stirring, until the sugar is dissolved. Add the chocolate pieces to the sugar mixture and stir until the chocolate has melted. Put the candy thermometer into the mixture and cook to 236 degrees.

  Take the saucepan off the heat. Add the butter or margarine, but don't stir it. Let the fudge cool until the bottom of the pan feels comfortably warm. The syrup cools very slowly, so this may take forty-five minutes or more. Meanwhile, lightly grease a pie pan or deep plate with butter or margarine.

  Stir in the vanilla. Then beat the fudge as hard as you can. It will already be quite stiff. Pour it into the pie pan or plate. It will start to harden immediately. Before the fudge is completely hard, cut it into squares. For easier cutting, warm the knife blade by dipping it into hot water; wipe the blade dry and cut the fudge into about thirty-six squares.

Chocolate Fudge II
(with marshmallow)

Follow the recipe for Chocolate Fudge I on page 63 *except* add about ½ cup marshmallow topping with the butter or margarine. This fudge hardens slowly.

Chocolate Fudge III
(with cocoa)

You will need measuring cups and spoons, a deep saucepan (2-quart size), potholder, wooden mixing spoon, candy thermometer, pie pan or deep plate, knife, and:

2 cups sugar
½ cup unsweetened cocoa powder
⅔ cup milk
¼ cup butter or margarine
1 teaspoon vanilla
  additional butter or margarine

Put the sugar and cocoa in the saucepan (a deep one because the mixture boils up quite high). Mix them thoroughly. Add the milk slowly, stirring to blend. Heat the mixture, stirring, until the sugar is dissolved and it starts to boil. Put the candy thermometer into the mixture and cook to 234 degrees.

Take the saucepan off the heat. Then follow the directions for Chocolate Fudge I on page 63.

Chocolate Fudge IV
(with brown sugar)

You will need measuring cups and spoons, a small saucepan, potholder, mixing spoon, candy thermometer, pie pan or deep plate, knife, and:

- 1 cup white sugar
- 1 cup brown sugar, firmly packed
- 2 tablespoons plus 1 teaspoon unsweetened cocoa powder
- ¼ cup milk
- ¼ cup light corn syrup
- ¼ cup butter or margarine
- 1 teaspoon vanilla
- additional butter or margarine

Put the sugars and cocoa powder in the saucepan. Mix them thoroughly. Add the milk slowly, stirring to blend. Add the corn syrup and the butter, cut into small pieces. Heat the mixture, stirring, until the sugar is dissolved and it starts to boil. Put the candy thermometer into the mixture and cook to 238 degrees. This candy cooks quickly; it will take only a few minutes to reach that temperature.

Take the saucepan off the heat and stir the mixture briskly until it is creamy. Stir in the vanilla.

Lightly grease a pie pan or deep plate with butter or margarine and pour the fudge into it. Let it cool for about forty-five minutes. When it has set enough to cut but is not yet completely hard, cut the fudge into thirty-six squares with a knife.

Chocolate Fudge V
(easy cooking)

You will need measuring cups and spoons, a small saucepan, potholder, mixing spoon, clock or watch (thermometer not needed), pie pan or deep plate, knife, and:

    ¾ cup sugar
    ½ cup evaporated milk
    ⅓ cup marshmallow topping
    1 tablespoon butter or margarine
    1 cup (6-ounce package) semisweet
       chocolate bits
    1 teaspoon vanilla
      additional butter or margarine

Put the sugar and milk in the saucepan. Add the marshmallow topping and butter or margarine. Heat, stirring constantly as the mixture starts to boil. Cook for exactly *five minutes*, STIRRING RAPIDLY. If you stop stirring for even a few seconds, it will scorch.

When the five minutes are up, take the saucepan off the heat and add the chocolate bits. Stir until the chocolate is melted and the mixture is smooth. Add the vanilla. Pour the mixture into the pan or plate that has been greased with butter or margarine and cool in the refrigerator. When set, cut the fudge into twenty-five squares.

Chocolate Fudge VI
(easiest of all)

You will need measuring cups and spoons, a small saucepan, mixing spoon, pie pan or plate, knife, and:

    ½ cup sweetened condensed milk
    1 cup (6-ounce package) semisweet chocolate bits
    1 tablespoon butter or margarine
    ½ teaspoon vanilla
    additional butter or margarine

Lightly grease the pie pan or deep plate with butter or margarine.

Put the condensed milk, chocolate bits, and butter or margarine in the saucepan. With the burner turned on very low, stir the mixture gently as the chocolate bits melt. When the mixture is smooth, add the vanilla. Pour it into the greased pan. Refrigerate for two hours. Cut the fudge into twenty-five squares.

Chocolate Plus Coconut

Using ready-made plain chocolate, like the semisweet chocolate bits or a plain chocolate bar, is a quick and convenient way to make your own chocolate candy.

You will need measuring cups and spoons, a small saucepan, mixing spoon, teaspoon, wax paper, and:

    1 cup (6-ounce package) semisweet chocolate bits
    ¼ cup light corn syrup
    2 teaspoons water
    1 teaspoon vanilla
    2 cups shredded coconut

Put the chocolate, corn syrup, and water in a saucepan. With the burner turned on very low, stir the mixture gently as the chocolate melts. When the mixture is smooth, take the saucepan off the heat.

Stir in the vanilla and the coconut. Drop by spoonfuls on a piece of wax paper. Chill in the refrigerator to harden the chocolate. This recipe makes about sixteen candies.

Chocolate Plus Cereal

Follow the recipe for Chocolate Plus Coconut on page 68 *except* use two cups of any plain dry cereal in place of the coconut.

Chocolate Plus Nuts

Follow the recipe for Chocolate Plus Coconut on page 68 *except* use two cups of any kind of chopped nuts in place of the coconut.

Chocolate Plus Plus

Follow the recipe for Chocolate Plus Coconut on page 68 *except* use two cups of any combination of cereal, nuts, coconut, seeds, etc., instead of all coconut.

Making chocolate-covered candy—called "dipped chocolates" in the trade—is a tricky business that requires perfect temperature control and a special knack. Chocolate is a fragile substance that must be handled carefully.

First the chocolate is melted to a maximum temperature of 140 degrees; at higher temperatures the chocolate may form lumps. Chocolate cannot stand the presence of even a drop of moisture, which causes it to harden immediately and become unworkable. Next the melted chocolate is pre-cooled by spreading and working it with a spatula or with the fingers until it is a little cooler than body temperature. This process keeps the fats and oils from separating out and forming gray streaks, called "bloom." The cooled chocolate is then "seeded" with finely grated cold chocolate. This seed chocolate contains unmelted cocoa butter that, when mixed with the melted chocolate, will help it to set up, or harden, properly. The whole process of heating, cooling, and seeding is called tempering.

Now the tempered chocolate is ready for dipping—fondants, caramels, or nuts, for instance. The candy-maker takes a center and dips it quickly into the melted chocolate, using either the fingers or a special dipping fork, and then puts it on a tray to set up, adding the distinctive little swirl on top that is part decoration and part identification. If the chocolate is too warm and runny or there is too much chocolate on the piece, it may form a pool around the piece. Or if the chocolate was not correctly tempered, it may not harden properly. Meanwhile, the chocolate must

Xocolatl to Chocolate 71

be kept at just the right temperature for dipping—neither too hot and runny nor too cool and thick.

All of this takes skill and practice. Although all chocolate-covered candy was once made this way by people skilled in the craft, today most of it is made in *enrobers,* in which the candy centers are carried on a moving belt through a curtain of liquid chocolate, which deposits an even coating on it. In another method, the chocolate shell is first formed in a mold and then filled.

Still want to try? Here's an easy recipe. Even if it doesn't look professional, it will taste fine.

Quick Chocolate Dips

You will need a double boiler, wooden mixing spoon, two baking sheets, wax paper, and:

    semisweet chocolate bits *or* 1 or 2 plain chocolate bars broken into pieces

    large whole nuts *or* Easy Fondant Patties (recipe on page 54)

Put the chocolate pieces in the upper part of the double boiler. Fill the lower part with enough hot water to touch the bottom and sides of the upper part. Set the upper part in place and cover it with a lid. Check after ten minutes; most of the chocolate should be melted. Stir it gently with a spoon, being careful not to get any moisture into the chocolate.

Spread a few spoons of the melted chocolate on a baking sheet. Stir it around with your fingers until it has cooled enough so that it feels neither warm nor cool but just about body temperature. (Put the rest of the chocolate over the hot water again to keep it warm.)

Dip each nut or fondant patty or piece of caramel into the chocolate, turning it so that it is completely covered. Let the excess chocolate drip back onto the pool of melted chocolate. Set the dipped candy on a baking sheet covered with wax paper. At this moment, professionals make the characteristic swirl with their fingertips on the top of the candy.

If the chocolate starts to get too stiff for dipping, add another spoonful of warm chocolate from the double boiler and work it in with your fingers.

When you have done a few, put them in the refrigerator for ten minutes to set up.

8
World Candy Sampler

People everywhere like sweet things. But some people like them sweeter than others do. And so candy made in different parts of the world reflects the local taste for sweetness and the kind of ingredients that are available, as well as custom and tradition. Some candies resemble our own favorites, but others seem strange and unusual and are very difficult to duplicate.

The people of India are fond of very sweet things, and they often *begin* as well as end their meals with something sweet. One favorite kind of Indian candy is *gulab jamun*, which is made by first boiling milk for hours to form a stiff dough, then deep-frying cardamom-flavored balls made of the dough, and finally soaking the fried balls in a heavy syrup. It's not something easily made at home, and there is nothing like it in our country.

In the Middle East, a kind of taffy dyed bright shades of red or blue is shaped in fat rings that are sold by candy vendors in the marketplaces. *Halvah,* a Turkish combination of semolina or farina flour with oil and sugar, is sometimes sold in American stores. But jellied cubes coated with sugar, called *lokum* in Turkey and Turkish Delight in this country, can be made easily in an American kitchen.

Turkish Delight

You will need measuring cups, a teacup, deep saucepan, potholder, wooden mixing spoon, candy thermometer, square glass or metal pan, sharp knife, wax paper, and:

    1 package unflavored gelatin
    ¼ cup cold water
    1 cup sugar
    1 package flavored gelatin dessert (orange, lemon, strawberry, etc.)
    1 cup hot water
    additional sugar

Chill the pan in the refrigerator while you cook the candy.

Mix the unflavored gelatin with the cold water in a teacup and let it soften.

Put the sugar, flavored gelatin dessert, and hot water in a deep saucepan. Heat them, stirring, until the mixture starts to boil. Put the candy thermometer into the mixture and cook to 222 degrees. Take the saucepan off the heat.

Add the softened gelatin to the cooked syrup and stir. Pour the syrup into the chilled pan. Allow to cool. Then put the pan of syrup into the refrigerator for about two hours, or until the syrup has become quite stiff and firm.

Dip a knife in hot water and run it around the edges of the pan to loosen the candy. Run an inch of hot water into the sink and dip the bottom of the pan into the water for no more than a minute to loosen the candy.

Sprinkle sugar on a piece of wax paper. Lift the candy out of the pan in one piece and lay it on the sugar. Sprinkle more sugar on top of it. Cut the candy in thirty-six cubes and roll them in sugar so that they are sanded on all sides. Store in a cool dry place.

The carob is an evergreen tree that grows near the Mediterranean and also the Caribbean. It produces edible pods, sometimes known as locust beans. The pods are also called St. John's bread, because of the Biblical story of John the Baptist who lived on honey and locusts, although the Bible referred to insects, not to beans. The pods have a rather sweet, chocolaty flavor, and the ground pods resemble cocoa powder. Sold in health-food stores as a chocolate substitute, carob is rich in protein and natural sugar, and it can be used to make a nutritious fudge. Don't expect it to taste *exactly* like chocolate, though, or you will be disappointed.

Carob

Carob Fudge

Follow the directions for Chocolate Fudge III on page 64 or Chocolate Fudge IV on page 66 *except* use carob powder instead of cocoa powder.

Some of the most elaborate candies in the world come from Latin America, where sugar grows abundantly in most countries. The art of candymaking is an old tradition among the nuns of Latin America. The idea of *dulces,* as the elegant confections are called, was imported from the convents of Spain soon after the arrival of the Spanish conquistadors. Today, in Lima, Peru, there is a convent that has the reputation for producing the most beautiful *dulces* in South America. Orphan girls are brought up there by the nuns, who teach them the confectioner's art.

But Latin America also has some very simple candies that date back centuries. Before the arrival of sugar cane from Spain, the Mexican Indians kept bees. The early Peruvians dried squash and sweet potatoes in the sun to make sweets. Today, sweet potatoes are ground to a paste and then flavored and colored to make the base for fancy candies. The seeds of the squash are treated in the same way; when the paste begins to harden, it is formed into elaborate shapes and decorated.

Candied vegetables and fruits are everywhere. You can try making some yourself, simmering slices in a thick sugar syrup, letting them dry, and rolling them in more sugar.

Candied Vegetables

You will need a measuring cup, small saucepan, vegetable peeler, sharp knife, cutting board, wire rack, slotted spoon, wax paper, and:

        vegetables to make 3 cups, sliced
     1 cup sugar
     ½ cup water

    Pick hard-fleshed vegetables such as carrots, pumpkin, winter squash, and sweet potatoes. Peel the vegetables and, using a sharp knife on a wooden cutting board, cut the vegetables in thin slices. The pieces will shrink as they cook, depending on their natural water content. Slice enough to make three cups.

    Put the sugar and water in the saucepan. Heat, stirring, until the mixture starts to boil. Turn down the heat and cook gently for fifteen minutes.

    Add the vegetable slices to the syrup and cook gently for about fifteen minutes or until they are tender when you poke them with the point of a sharp knife.

World Candy Sampler

Lift the slices out of the syrup with a slotted spoon and spread them out to dry on a wire rack with a piece of wax paper spread underneath it to catch the drips.

After the vegetable slices have dried for several hours, roll them in more sugar, which has been sprinkled on another sheet of wax paper. Put them back on the rack to dry thoroughly.

Candied Coconut

You may need someone to help you with the coconut. First, drill two holes in the "eyes" of the coconut and drain out the liquid. Heat the oven to 350 degrees and bake the coconut for twenty minutes. Then bounce the coconut a few times on a hard floor to loosen the coconut meat. Use a hammer or mallet to crack open the coconut and break it into pieces. Pull the coconut meat away from the shell. With a sharp knife carefully peel off the brown skin. Slice the coconut meat into strips.

Follow the directions in the Candied Vegetables recipe on page 78 for preparing the syrup and cooking the coconut strips until they look translucent. Follow the same recipe for drying and sugaring the coconut.

Molasses Taffy

One of the simplest candies to make originates in Puerto Rico, where molasses is plentiful.

You will need a measuring cup, saucepan, potholder, candy thermometer, large platter or baking sheet, scissors or knife, wax paper or plastic wrap, and:

>about 1 cup molasses
>butter or margarine
>cornstarch

Put the molasses in a deep saucepan, put the candy thermometer into it, and cook to 270 degrees.

Grease a platter or baking sheet with butter or margarine and pour the cooked molasses onto it.

When the molasses is cool enough to handle, grease your hands and pull the molasses like taffy (see page 51) until it is golden brown. Twist it into a rope and cut it in about three dozen pieces with scissors or a knife dipped in cornstarch. Wrap each piece separately in wax paper or plastic wrap.

Nuts are almost as important in candymaking as sugar and chocolate. Although you can make many kinds of candy without nuts, they do transform ordinary candy into something special, and in some candies nuts are one of the main ingredients.

Marzipan, one of the earliest candies, is made with ground almonds. In France, almonds and pistachios are mixed with a sweet candy base to make *nougat*, although walnuts were originally used. (*Nougat* is derived from the Latin word for walnut, *nux*.) The

World Candy Sampler

Italian version of nougat is called *torrone*. The most popular kind, *Torrone di Cremona*, was supposedly made by the monks in the bell tower *(torre)* of the cathedral in Cremona.

Although nougat and torrone are delicious, they are difficult to make. Divinity is the heaven-inspired name of a somewhat similar American candy that is much easier to make.

Divinity

You will need measuring cups and spoons, a mixing bowl, small saucepan, potholder, wooden mixing spoon, candy thermometer, electric mixer, wax paper, and:

    1 egg white
   1⅓ cups sugar
    ⅓ cup light corn syrup
    ¼ cup water
    1 teaspoon vanilla
    ½ cup chopped nuts

Egg white is easier to beat when it is at room temperature. If you are in a hurry, put the whole egg in a cup of warm water for a few minutes. Separate the white from the yolk very carefully; if any of the yolk gets in the white, the white will not beat properly. Start over with another egg if necessary. Put the egg white in the mixing bowl. Store the egg yolk in a covered jar with a little cold water and use it in scrambled eggs or another recipe.

Meanwhile, put the sugar, corn syrup, and water in a saucepan. Heat them, stirring, until the mixture starts to boil. Put the candy thermometer into the mixture and cook to 256 degrees.

While the syrup is boiling, beat the egg white with the electric mixer. Beat it until it is very stiff. Keep one eye on the thermometer while you beat.

Then slowly pour the hot syrup into the egg white, in a thin stream, beating all the time you are pouring. Keep beating until the mixture is no longer shiny. By then it will be very stiff.

Mix in the vanilla and chopped nuts and drop the divinity by spoonfuls on the wax paper. You will have about eighteen candies.

Sea Foam

Sea foam is like Divinity, except that it is made with brown sugar instead of white.

You will need measuring cups and spoons, a mixing bowl, small saucepan, potholder, wooden mixing spoon, candy thermometer, electric mixer, wax paper, and:

  1 egg white
  1½ cups light brown sugar, firmly packed
  ¼ cup water
  1 tablespoon light corn syrup
  1 teaspoon vanilla
  ½ cup chopped nuts

Follow the directions for Divinity on page 82.

Pralines

In the seventeenth century, the chef of a famous French diplomat assured his employer, *le comte du Plessis-Praslin,* that almonds coated with sugar syrup would not upset his delicate stomach. In France, *pralines,* as they were called, are made with almonds and white sugar, but when the idea was imported to Louisiana by the French settlers, the cooks substituted plentiful local pecans for the almonds and brown sugar for white.

You will need measuring cups and spoons, small saucepan, potholder, wooden mixing spoon, candy thermometer, wax paper, and:

    2 cups light brown sugar, firmly packed
    3 tablespoons water
    2 teaspoons butter or margarine
    1 cup pecans, whole or chopped

Put the sugar, water, and butter or margarine into the saucepan. Heat them, stirring, until the mixture starts to boil. Put the candy thermometer into the mixture and cook to 238 degrees. Take the saucepan off the heat.

Add the nuts and stir hard until the mixture is thick. Drop by spoonfuls on a sheet of wax paper to make about eighteen pralines.

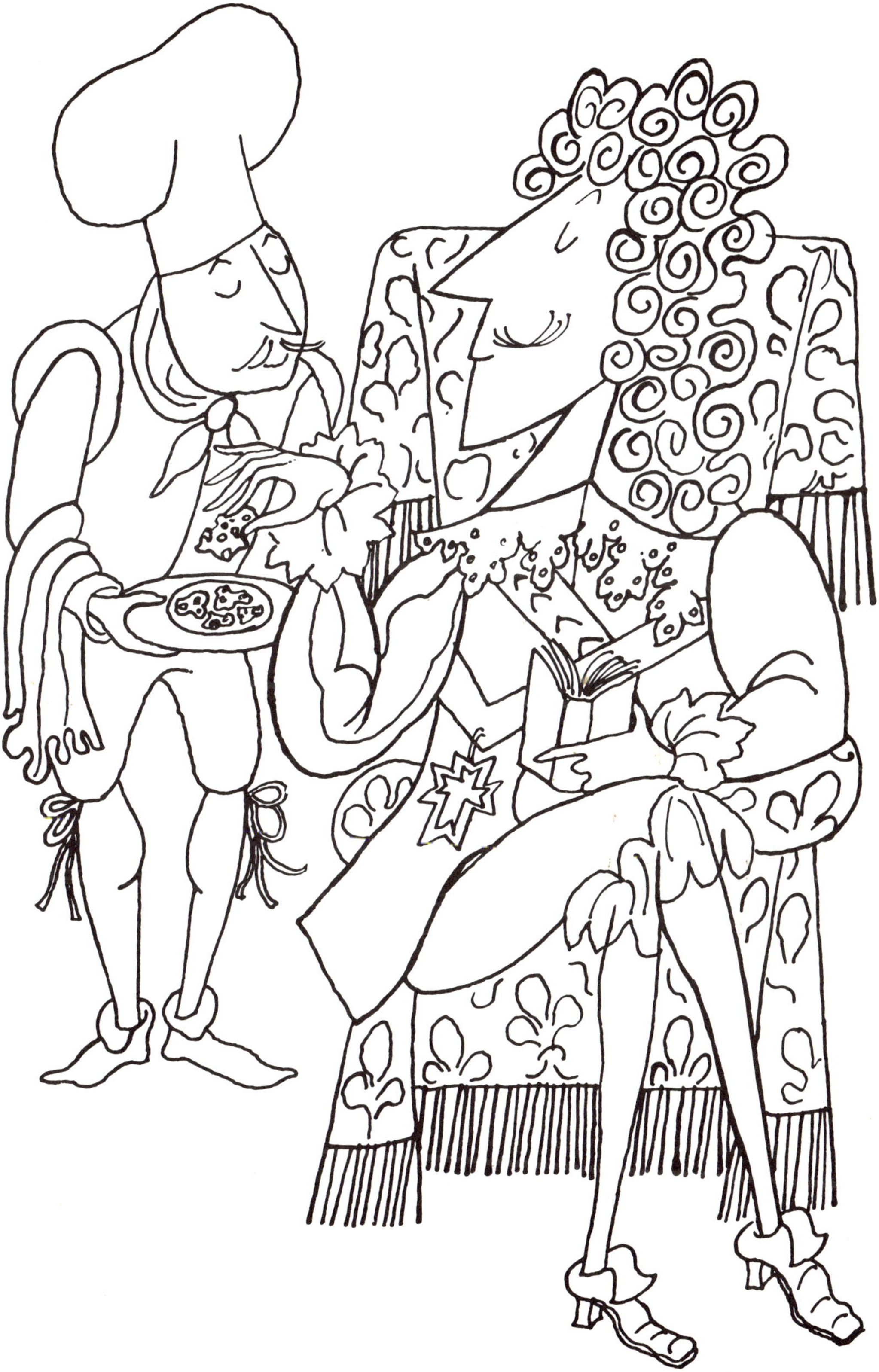

Peanut Brittle

Peanuts were first grown by the Indians of South America, before the arrival of Columbus. Called groundnuts in Africa, where they were later grown, peanuts were eventually brought to North America along with the first African slaves. Groundnuts are used by African cooks to make a candy that is much like the old American favorite, peanut brittle.

World Candy Sampler

You will need measuring cups and spoons, a saucepan, potholder, wooden mixing spoon, candy thermometer, baking sheet, and:

- 1 cup sugar
- ¼ cup water
- ½ cup light corn syrup
- 1 teaspoon butter or margarine
- 1 cup or 6-ounce package salted roasted peanuts
- ½ teaspoon baking soda
- ½ teaspoon vanilla
  additional butter or margarine

Lightly grease a baking sheet with butter or margarine.

Put the sugar, water, corn syrup, and butter or margarine in the saucepan. Heat them, stirring, until the mixture starts to boil. Put the candy thermometer into the mixture and cook to 300 degrees. Cook another minute or two, until it begins to turn golden brown.

Take the saucepan off the heat. Stir in the peanuts, then the baking soda, and then the vanilla.

Pour the peanut mixture on the baking sheet. It will already be starting to harden. Spread as thin as possible with the mixing spoon so the peanuts are only one layer thick. As it cools and before it hardens completely, pull on the edges so the candy will be very thin.

When the peanut brittle is hard (and it will really be "brittle"), break it into pieces and store it in a tightly covered container.

Peanut Butter Fudge

You will need measuring cups, a deep saucepan, potholder, mixing spoon, candy thermometer, pie pan or deep plate, sharp knife, and:

    1 cup sugar
    ½ cup milk
    ½ cup marshmallow topping
    ½ cup peanut butter, chunk-style
      butter or margarine

Put the sugar and milk in a deep saucepan. Heat them, stirring, until the mixture starts to boil. Put the candy thermometer into the mixture and cook to 236 degrees.

Take the saucepan off the heat and add the marshmallow topping and peanut butter. Stir it in gently. Let it cool until the bottom of the pan feels comfortably warm.

Meanwhile, lightly grease with butter or margarine a pie pan or deep plate. Beat the fudge and pour it into the pan or plate. Chill in the refrigerator for a few hours. Then cut the fudge in about twenty-five squares with a sharp knife.

Toffee is sometimes described as the British cousin of American caramel, but actually it falls somewhere between caramel and peanut brittle—harder than chewy caramel, softer than crunchy peanut brittle. Toffee is made with lots of butter, and an even richer version of it calls for a chocolate and nut coating. Try making caramels first. Then go on to one of the two kinds of toffee.

World Candy Sampler

Caramels

You will need measuring cups and spoons, a deep saucepan, potholder, wooden mixing spoon, candy thermometer, large pie pan, sharp knife, wax paper or plastic wrap, and:

    1 cup sugar
    1 cup light corn syrup
    ¼ cup butter or margarine
    ¾ cup evaporated milk
       additional butter or margarine
    1 teaspoon vanilla

If the evaporated milk is not at room temperature, put it in a cup or glass and set it in a bowl of hot water for a few minutes. Keep it near the stove.

Put the sugar and corn syrup in a saucepan. Heat them, stirring, until the mixture starts to boil. Put the candy thermometer into the mixture and cook to 250 degrees.

Cut the butter or margarine into small pieces. When the syrup has cooked, remove the candy thermometer and lay it aside, but keep it close by. Add the butter or margarine a piece at a time, stirring with the wooden spoon while it melts. Make sure the mixture keeps on boiling.

After the butter or margarine pieces have been added, pour the milk in very slowly, a little at a time, so that the mixture keeps on boiling. Stir constantly with the wooden spoon.

Cook the mixture for ten minutes, stirring rapidly. The milk will scorch if you don't stir steadily and cover all parts of the bottom of the pan.

After ten minutes, lay aside the mixing spoon and quickly begin to stir with the candy thermometer. When the thermometer reads 245 degrees, take the saucepan off the heat.

While the mixture cools slightly, grease a large pie pan. Stir the vanilla flavoring into the caramel mixture and pour the mixture into the pie pan. Cool at room temperature until the bottom of the pan feels just warm. Then refrigerate for several hours.

Put the bottom of the pie pan in hot water or on a warm burner for a minute or two to loosen the caramel. Then turn it upside down on a cutting board so that the slab of caramel drops out. Cut the candy first in strips, and then in about fifty squares. Wrap each square separately.

Almond Toffee

You will need measuring cups and spoons, a small saucepan, potholder, wooden mixing spoon, candy thermometer, baking sheet, knife, and:

⅔ cup butter or margarine
½ cup sugar
⅓ cup water
⅔ cup (3-ounce package) blanched almonds, whole or pieces
¼ teaspoon baking soda

Put the butter or margarine, sugar, and water in a small saucepan. Heat them, stirring, until the butter is melted and the mixture starts to boil. Put the candy thermometer into the mixture and cook to 236 degrees.

Add the almonds. Use the thermometer as a paddle to stir—frequently at first, and then constantly as the mixture gets thick and golden and the almonds toast to a light brown. Cook to 290 degrees. Take the saucepan off the heat and add the baking soda.

Pour the toffee on the baking sheet, using a knife to shape the batch into a rectangle and smooth out the nuts. When the toffee has cooled but is still soft, use a knife to press lines into it, scoring the toffee into about twenty-four squares or rectangles. When it is cool, break the pieces apart along the scored lines.

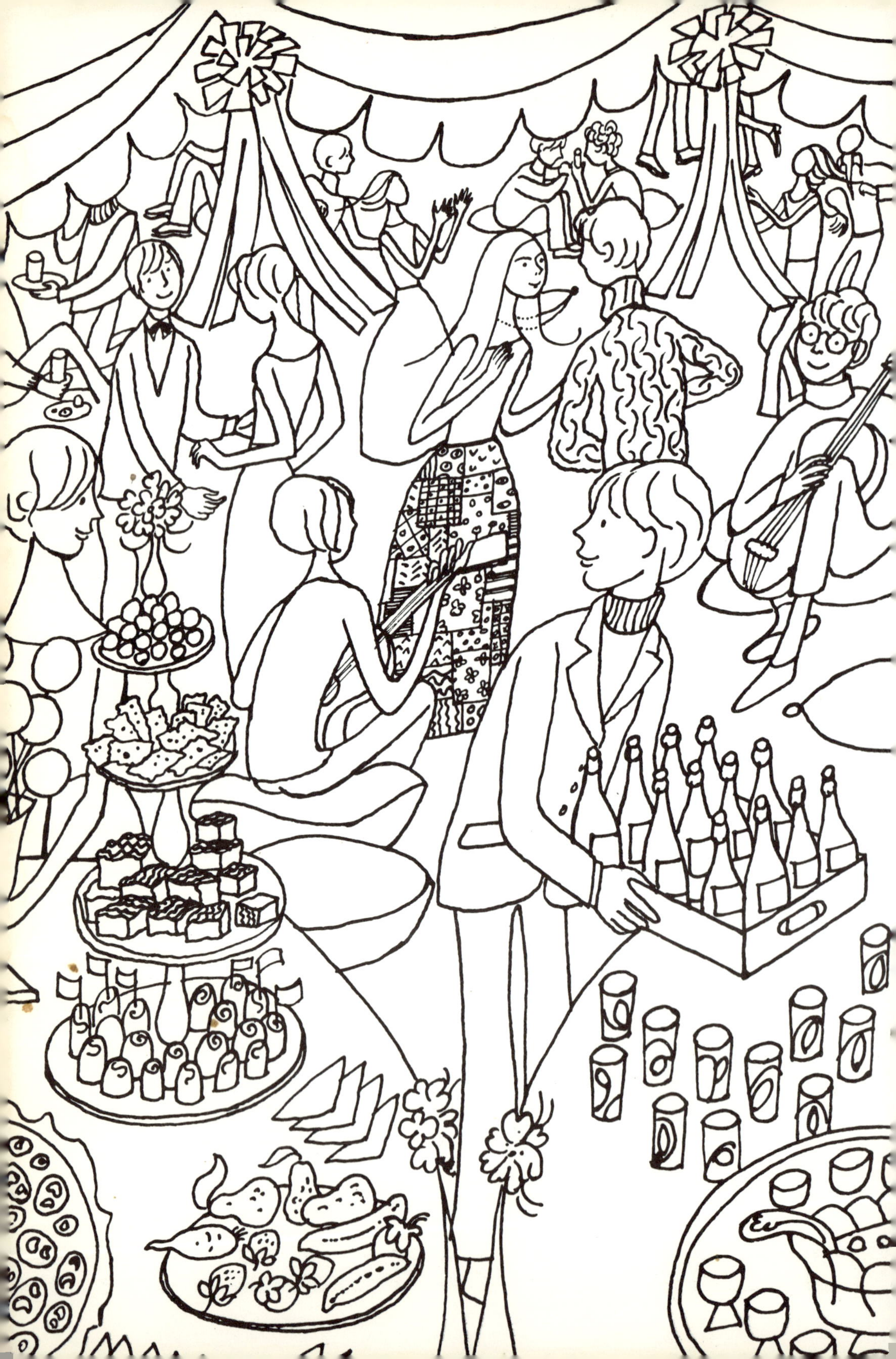

World Candy Sampler

Super Toffee

Follow the recipe for Almond Toffee on page 91 *except* you will also need aluminum foil and:

    1 cup (6-ounce package) semisweet chocolate bits
    ½ cup chopped pecans

After you have made the toffee rectangle on the baking sheet, sprinkle it with the chocolate bits. Cover the toffee with a sheet of aluminum foil so that the heat of the toffee will melt the chocolate.

After a few minutes, use the back of the mixing spoon to spread the melted chocolate evenly over the rectangle, and sprinkle it with chopped pecans. Press the pecans lightly into the soft chocolate.

Use a knife to press lines into the soft toffee, scoring it into about twenty-four squares or rectangles. When completely cooled, break it apart along the scored lines. Wrap each piece in aluminum foil.

If you have made all, or even most, of the candy in this book, you are well on the way to becoming an expert candymaker. As a treat for you and your family you can make candy for everyday use or for holidays and special occasions. You can make it for fund-raising fairs and bazaars or use it as a way of earning extra money for yourself. You can turn candymaking into a party, as many people did in the early days of this country, when cooking fudge or pulling taffy was an evening's entertainment.

And you can please someone you like a lot with a box of lots and lots of candy that you've made yourself.

Index

All numbers in boldface indicate recipes.

Africa, 19, 58, 86
Alexander the Great, 16
Almond paste, 22
Almond Toffee, **91**
America, 7, 8, 13, 26, 58, 74, 86, 88
Apothecaries, 19, 20
Apple Slices, Candied, **33-34**
Aztecs, 7, 56, 58

Bees, 11-12, 27, 77
Bible, 12, 76
Brown sugar, 29
Brown Sugar Popcorn Balls, **40**

Cacao, 56-58
Candied Apple Slices, **33-34**
Candied Cereals, **41**
Candied Coconut, **79**
Candied Vegetables, **78**
Candy bars, 8, 13, 18, 61
Candy Circles, Clear, **44-45**
Candymaking, commercial, 7, 8, 13, 20-21, 26, 30, 60-61, 70-71, 77
Candy thermometer, 9-10, 43
Caramel Popcorn, **38-39**
Caramels, **89-90**
Carbohydrate(s), 28, 29, 30
Caribbean, 18, 19, 20, 76
Carob, 76

Carob Fudge, **77**
Cereal(s)
　Candied, **41**
　Chocolate Plus, **69**
　Marzipan, **23**
Chocolate, 7, 8, 56-62, 70-72, 76, 80
　dipped, 8, 70-71, **72**
　Plus Cereal, **69**
　Plus Coconut, **68-69**
　Plus Nuts, **69**
　Plus Plus, **69**
Chocolate Fudge
　I, with unsweetened chocolate, **63**
　II, with marshmallow, **64**
　III, with cocoa, **64-65**
　IV, with brown sugar, **66**
　V, easy cooking, **67**
　VI, easiest of all, **68**
Cocoa, 60, 76, 77
Cocoa butter, 60
Coconut
　Candied, **79**
　Chocolate Plus, **68-69**
　-Molasses Candy, **32**
Columbus, 18, 56, 86
Confectioners, 20
Corn syrup, 43-44
Cortez, 7, 56-57
Cream Cheese Filling, **35**
Crusaders, 17, 18, 19, 21

Index

Denmark, 21
Diet, 28, 30
Divinity, 81, **82-83**
Dulces, 77

Egypt, ancient, 12-13, 17
Elizabeth I of England, 29
England, 8, 26, 29, 58, 88
Europe, 7, 17-18, 19, 20, 21, 57

Fondant Patties, Easy, **54-55**
France, 26, 57, 80, 84
Fructose, 27
Fruits, candied, 77
Fudge, 43, 44, 61-62
    Carob, **77**
    Chocolate I, with unsweetened chocolate, **63**
    Chocolate II, with marshmallow, **64**
    Chocolate III, with cocoa, **64-65**
    Chocolate IV, with brown sugar, **66**
    Chocolate V, easy cooking, **67**
    Chocolate VI, easiest of all, **68**
    Peanut Butter, **88**
    Penuche, **47**
    Vanilla Cream, **46**

Germany, 21
Glucose, 27
Grain, 42-44
Gur, 17

Halvak, 74
Hershey Foods, 59-61
Honey, 7, 11-13, **14-15**, 16, 28, 29
    Balls, **14**
    Popcorn Balls, **36-37**
    Seed Candy, **15**

India, 16-17, 73
Italy, 21, 26, 81

Lollipops, 43, 44

Maple sugar and maple syrup, 26, 28
Marshmallows, **52-53**
Marzipan, 21-22, 80
    Cereal, **23**
    Miniatures, Potato, **25**
    Potato, **24-25**
Mediterranean, 17, 18
Mexico, 7, 47, 56, 77
Middle East, 13, 74
Molasses, 17, 28, 29
    -Coconut Candy, **32**
    Taffy, **80**
Montezuma, 56

Nougat, 80-81
Nuts, 8, 21, 80-81, **82-84**, **86-88**, **91**, **93**
    Chocolate Plus, **69**

Orient, 17, 21

Peanut Brittle, **86-87**
Peanut Butter Fudge, **88**
Penuche, **47**
Peru, 77
Peter, Daniel, 58
Pliny the Elder, 16

Popcorn Balls
  Brown Sugar, **40**
  Honey, **36-37**
  Sugar, **37-38**
Popcorn, Caramel, **38-39**
Portugal, 18, 34
Potato Marzipan Miniatures, **25**
Potato Marzipan Potatoes, **24-25**
Pralines, **84**
Prehistoric man, 11, 29

Rock Candy, Old-fashioned, **55**
Rome, ancient, 16, 17, 19

Safety precautions, 10
Sea Foam, **83**
Slave trade, 19
South America, 58, 77, 86
Spain, 7, 18, 56-57, 77
Sucrose, 27, 28

Sugar, 7, 16-21, 27-30, 42-44
Sugar beet, 27, 28
Sugar cane, 7, 16-17, 18-19, 27, 28, 77
Sugar maple, 28
Sugarplums, 34-35
Sugar Popcorn Balls, **37-38**
Sugar syrup, 42-44
Switzerland, 58

Taffy, 43, 44, 49-50, **50-51**
  Molasses, **80**
Toffee, 88
  Almond, **91**
  Super, **93**
Tooth decay, 29-30
Torrone, 81
Turbinado, 29
Turkish Delight, 74, **75-76**

Vanilla Cream Fudge, **46**
Vegetables, Candied, 77, **78-79**